UNbroken

A True Story of Hope in Starting Over

WENDY BAISLEY ROACHE

WESTBOW
PRESS®
A DIVISION OF THOMAS NELSON
& ZONDERVAN

This book is a work of non-fiction. Unless otherwise noted, the author
and the publisher make no explicit guarantees as to the accuracy of
the information contained in this book and in some cases, names of
people and places have been altered to protect their privacy.

WestBow Press books may be ordered through booksellers or by contacting:

WestBow Press
A Division of Thomas Nelson & Zondervan
1663 Liberty Drive
Bloomington, IN 47403
www.westbowpress.com
1 (866) 928-1240

All photos used in cover were taken by author and author's husband.

ISBN: 978-1-5127-1956-7 (sc)
ISBN: 978-1-5127-1955-0 (hc)
ISBN: 978-1-5127-1954-3 (e)

Library of Congress Control Number: 2015918670

Print information available on the last page.

WestBow Press rev. date: 11/20/2015

"Captivating" - If you have ever wondered why, or doubted that, God would allow the world to be so broken ... if you have hit the bottom so hard that you lost the desire to even try to get up and try again ... this book will speak to you. This story will lead you into the depths of human tragedy and despair and allow you to find your own way out as the main character finds her way out ... one cannot help but grow in faith through the powerful testimony of the author. A must read for anyone who has ever even slightly doubted that all things are possible with God.

~ Michael Wofford, PharmD.,
Department of Health Care Services

Wendy's story is an incredible testimony of triumph in the face of adversity. Readers will be captivated by the courage, hope, peace, and love that emanate through the pages as she recalls how God so graciously put her life back together after devastating heartbreak. She tells her story with great boldness and courage and I truly believe that every reader will be touched by UNbroken.

~ Matthew Barnett, Cofounder of The Dream Center

Inspiring and offering hope for the deepest of hurts. UNbroken is a captivating read depicting beauty from ashes. Presented in a real and raw form that breaks down the stereotypes of who the broken are, giving hope to us all. Authentic and sure to speak hope and healing into many who feel they are beyond grace and redemption.

~ Shannon Bezak, Hope House Director

UNbroken is the poignant story of Wendy's courageous recovery from a devastating, personal betrayal. Out of her deep anguish, a life of prayer is born that finds miraculous answers coming to her through the loving providence of God. She shares with great transparency how this experience of the love of God embraces her heart with compassionate healing, enables her to forgive her transgressors and empowers her to rebuild her life. Hers is a vivid testimony to the transforming power of love. A love that permeates these pages and will surely touch your life as it did mine!

~ Ed Piorek, Pastor and Author of *The Father Loves You*

Have you ever wondered how God could pursue you after you've faced the deepest levels of brokenness, pain and a life spent running from His love? Wendy's story will reveal the power of God's love and how no one is beyond rescue and restoration. This gripping story of abuse, betrayal and unthinkable pain will give every hopeless heart a reason to believe that there is a road out and a life of wholeness and purpose found in Christ. "UNbroken" is a worthwhile read that will ignite every heart to truly believe that he gives "a crown of beauty for our ashes and a garment of praise in exchange for our despair" (Isaiah 61:3). This book will inspire you to fall upon the grace and strength of God no matter the pain or brokenness of your past; He can use your life for His glory!

~ David Patterson, Lead Pastor, The Father's House

"Encouraging and Inspirational" - A real page turner. I was so blessed by this book I want to share it with others. Wendy put into practice the scripture 1 Thessalonians 5:16-18 to Rejoice Always and as she trusted and praised God, He used this thankful spirit for her good.

~ Joann Carothers Thomas & Foundation of Praise Staff

Reading UNbroken sparked a hope in me to trust God more with my life. I found myself tearing up over and over again at God's miraculous love and rescue from hopelessness. This book shows how turning to God can take a shattered and broken life and turn it into a thing of beauty. Every story and chapter inspired me to let go of my fears, my past, and to put complete trust in the Lord for my future.

~ Susanne Johnson, Police Special Services

Wendy's life journey reminds me of the Hebrews living in Egypt in the days of Moses. They underwent traumatic experiences as helpless slaves. As they cried to God for help, God heard their groaning and sent Moses to rescue and liberate them. He protected them and exposed them to His laws as He prepared them to enter the Promised Land. It seems that is what God has done in Wendy's life! He snatched her from bondage and mercifully revealed Himself to her through His living word. It is my hope and prayer that Wendy's testimony be anointed by God's Spirit and alter the soul and spirit of the reader!

~ Eddy Swieson, Author of *Why The Angels Laughed* &
Commentary Writer for Community Bible Study (CBS)

Dedicated to my daughter, for her relentless determination and drive, her amazing strength and bravery, and the promise we made to each other that we would never let this pain be in vain but instead, use it for good. And to my son, for all his love and support and his ever determined desire to be a man of courage, kindness, and integrity.

Contents

Special Thanks.. xv
Introduction...xvii

Chapter 1   The Phone Call...1
Chapter 2   Swept Away 13
Chapter 3   The Light Bulb 19
Chapter 4   Facing the World 27
Chapter 5   Forgiveness 36
Chapter 6   Running for Cover...................................44
Chapter 7   Breaking Free 53
Chapter 8   Heading South 64
Chapter 9   A Cup of Coffee 71
Chapter 10   A Side of Job 79
Chapter 11   A Little House for Dessert 86
Chapter 12   The Oval Tub 92
Chapter 13   Riviera..101
Chapter 14   On My Knees 110
Chapter 15   Little Lamb...122
Chapter 16   Holding On 130
Chapter 17   The Power of a Promise.........................142
Chapter 18   Always a Choice.....................................160
Chapter 19   Beyond Broken 178

Epilogue 199

Special Thanks

First, to my children—thank you for your ongoing kindness and loving support in this endeavor.

To my parents, family, and friends—you are the ones who stood beside me along this path, helping me, boldly pushing me, feeding me encouraging words, and cheering me on along the way. I humbly thank you for your loving kindness; your endearing fortitude, prayers, and provision; and for all the time and energy you gave to my children and me, including your smiles, hugs, and the tissues needed along the way. I sincerely thank you for making such a positive impact in our lives.

Next, to those I know and to those I have never met who were willing to share their own true stories of hope—I thank you for making your experiences available, for I have been blessed. And to those who, through messages, teachings, written words, works of art, and numerous inspirational songs, have brought encouragement and lifted my spirits countless times—thank you for your faithfulness, for following your hearts, and for putting your trust in God by willingly sharing the gifts you were given. I am eternally grateful for your commitment to spreading the good news. You have made a significant difference in the world at large and, most especially, in mine.

Also, to my wonderfully caring and generous new husband, whose love and support are the reasons why this book is possible—thank you for believing in me and providing for me and for your gracious kindness and remarkable patience in allowing me the time to finish this quest. I truly love, respect, and appreciate you.

Finally, to my Lord and Savior who gave his all for me, who never stopped pursuing me, and who waited patiently for me to choose him—thank you, Lord, for loving me and for always remaining a choice for me.

Introduction

This is a true story. Names have been altered to respect the privacy of those individuals included in this journey. As in every situation, each person has a story to tell of how events directly affected his or her personal life; this story tells mine ... and how, in the midst of life stripping things away, God was busy rebuilding.

The inspiration to begin writing this book came after finding a little note I had written years earlier—and right after losing everything—that read: "All I want in life is a cup of coffee, with a side of job and a little house for dessert." Although this account speaks of my own personal experience, I do not want this story to be so much about who I am or about any other character portrayed here but about who God is and what he can do with someone like me.

Now to you, the reader—this story is about truth, and like all truth, it will be harsh. But it will also inspire. I challenge you to persevere through my story of unimaginable loss and betrayal because you will soon see the freedom and victory found through God's grace and the very reason we all can have hope.

Chapter 1

The Phone Call

It was Monday, July 1, and with only ten minutes remaining in my workday, I rushed around frantically, finishing up a few last-minute details before heading off on vacation for the remainder of the week.

Suddenly, the new receptionist was standing at my desk. "I have a call for you," she said.

"Go ahead and transfer it to my desk, please," I requested.

"I can't," she replied. "It's the police department, and they said they need to talk to you. They said it's very important, and I'm afraid I might disconnect your call. Will you please come to the front desk to take this call?"

Panicked thoughts filled my head as I walked quickly toward the front office, dodging other staff along the way. What if something was wrong with my children or my husband? I anxiously picked up the blinking phone line at the receptionist's desk. "Hello, this is Wendy. Can I help you?" I asked nervously.

"This is Sergeant Collins from the Cloverdale Police Department, and we need you to come down to the station immediately."

"Why?" I cried out. "What has happened?"

"It's your husband," the officer responded. "He's been arrested, along with another man." There was silence as I felt myself go lightheaded.

What? No! I thought, as I slowly sank into the receptionist's chair. I barely heard the officer continue.

"If you feel you cannot drive yourself, an officer will come and pick you up to bring you here. If you are able to drive, do not go to your house first, as an officer is waiting there and will not let you enter your home. You need to come directly to the station."

With my head spinning and fear gripping my heart, I raced back to my desk, mumbling "I don't understand!" over and over again. I quickly grabbed my purse and flew out the door. It didn't even dawn on me that I had just left an office of over eighty employees and never told a soul that I was leaving—although I'm sure the news traveled like a wildfire throughout the building within minutes.

As I drove to the local police station, my head was exploding with questions. "How could this be? He's at work two hundred miles away! He's a man of the law! He's too smart to do anything wrong!" I cried to myself as I drove. My husband, Lawrence, had just accepted a new position in a weapons unit at a law enforcement academy about two hundred miles north of where we were living. He had worked at the academy as a weapons instructor when we first met nine years earlier. He had been an officer for over twenty-nine years, and he was known for his pleasant disposition on the force, so much so that his coworkers called him "Soft Shoe." He could give someone a ticket and leave them happy to take it. All I could think was perhaps he and a coworker had been tempted to take a weapon instead of destroying it. "But he is too smart for that," I repeated over and over to myself.

We had been married seven and a half years to the day, and my husband and I had made plans months in advance to celebrate the Fourth of July week with friends on the water. I had stocked our boat with clothes, food, and supplies two days earlier. Lawrence had towed the boat north the day before and parked it near his office at the academy, ready to launch it in the nearby river. We had put our house on the market three days earlier, and Lawrence was staying with his daughter from an earlier marriage—she lived near the academy—until we could sell our home and relocate the family.

My son, Christopher, and daughter, Emily, from a previous marriage had left two weeks earlier on a three-week trip with their father, Mitch, and grandmother. The children's grandfather had passed away at the end of May, and Mitch wanted to take the children with him when he drove his mother to Oklahoma, where she planned on staying with her brother for a while. I didn't know how I was going to tell Christopher and Emily about their stepfather. What would I say when they returned? Christopher had always looked up to Lawrence; he would even put on pretend uniforms with a badge. The thought of telling Christopher that Lawrence may have done something wrong was crushing my heart to no end.

As I pulled into the police station's entrance, I realized I couldn't even recall the drive there. Confusing thoughts continued to leap through my mind as I remembered the last conversation I'd had with Lawrence. It was earlier that morning, at about eleven o'clock. I was busy working at my desk when my phone rang.

"Is everything okay? How are you doing?" he'd asked. His probing questions were more perplexing than comforting, as he'd asked the same thing in the last two calls I'd received from him—one at seven that morning and the other at eleven the night before. He didn't seem himself. It was as if something was troubling him. When I'd asked the same questions of him, he'd answered, "I'm fine," and "I'm sitting here all alone in the weapons unit." Then Lawrence went on to explain, "All the other officers were just called up to a meeting in the main administration building, so I have a little downtime and thought I would give you a call."

I shared my excitement about our boat trip and reminded him I would be boarding the train soon to meet him at the dock on the river. I could hardly wait to see him again. I was missing him and remembering that before he was transferred, a week didn't go by without his taking me to lunch or bringing me flowers.

As I entered the police station's lobby, my legs were shaking. Fear took hold and got the best of me. I trembled as I opened my mouth to give my name to the officer behind the counter; my voice was barely understandable.

"Please have a seat," the officer said. "The detective will be right with you."

As I turned to find a seat, I saw other people in the room and found myself quickly turning my face toward the floor out of shame and embarrassment. I could not understand what was happening. *We are good and ethical people*, I thought, *and we don't belong on this side of the counter.*

The detective quickly escorted me to a private office, where I was introduced to the sergeant. "Please have a seat," he said.

"I think I would rather stand," I replied, looking helplessly at him.

"No, you need to sit down before I tell you what I have to say," the sergeant said. The look on his face sent a shock through me. As I continued to look into the sergeant's eyes, I reached a hand behind me, stretching to find the chair, so I could slowly lower myself into it without falling. My heart was pounding, yet the sound of his voice was kind and gentle.

Another officer popped his head in the door and said, "They've arrived." The detective turned to the sergeant; they signaled something to each other, and then away the detective went with the other officer, quickly excusing himself from the room.

The sergeant stood in front of me and said bluntly, "Your husband has been arrested for the rape and molestation of your daughter for the past six years."

His words hit me like a bolt of lightning. I went numb all over, white blotches flashing before my eyes. If I hadn't already been sitting, I would have dropped to the floor. *When? How? Why? What?* Each question raced through my mind.

"Where is she?" I cried. "Where is my daughter? Is she okay?"

"She is with her father right now, along with your son. Child Protective Services released them into his custody."

I was in so much shock I could hardly breathe. Tears were running down my face; this news was so much worse than anything I had imagined on my way to the station. With the one ounce of breath I had left, I managed to squeak out another question. "Who is the other man, and why was he arrested?"

The sergeant looked at me and paused. "Regretfully," he said, "the other man is a friend of your husband's, a local businessman by the name of Branton, who joined in on the abuse over the past six months."

My heart sank even lower.

I immediately flashed back to thoughts of Branton—a boater as well and someone known for being a partier. His wife had left him a couple months earlier. She never said why; all I knew was that Branton had bought her a car, and she had packed it up and left town.

I had always been uncomfortable around him, and that thought haunted me. Flashes of memories came back to me, especially how I had insisted Christopher and Emily were not to be around Branton. I then remembered changes I had noticed in Lawrence's behavior over the past six to eight months, ever since he had been hanging out more with his friend. I distinctly remembered his taking me to Branton's home for dinner one Friday night after his wife left. When we walked into Branton's house, there was porn playing on a big-screen TV. I asked him to change the channel, but he laughed at me. He and Lawrence were both acting differently and pushing me to do things I didn't want to do. I ended up walking out of his house, alone. I was nine miles from home and on foot, but all I could think of was how badly I wanted to go home. A kindhearted couple noticed me weeping as I passed by their house and ran out to see if I needed help. I ended up using their telephone to call Lawrence, who picked me up and took me home.

The sergeant was watching me with concerned eyes as my mind spun in circles. Thoughts of earlier times in the year came to mind. I had been feeling like something was terribly wrong, but I hadn't been able to put my finger on it. For months I felt it in my gut, but I could never see it with my eyes. I tried and tried to figure it out, to the point where I felt like I was going crazy. When I confided in Lawrence, he said it was the stress of my job. He told me to decline the promotion that I had been offered. He told me I needed help, and he made an appointment for me to see a counselor, which I did. Even the counselor, Mr. Ellis, couldn't figure out the cause of my sickening gut and anxiety. And with that thought, I stood up from my chair, stared straight into the sergeant's eyes and cried out, "Now it all makes sense!" I repeated it over and over again as tears poured down my cheeks. "Sergeant, I knew something was wrong, but I never dreamed it had something to do with my daughter."

In a kind yet stern voice, the sergeant changed the subject by asking me for my house key. "We need to search your house for evidence," he informed me. "I would much rather use your key than break down your door. The officers are at your house right now, and they need to begin their search."

"Yes," I replied as I pulled the keys out of my purse. My hands were shaking as I tried to detach the house key from my key ring. Handing the key to the sergeant with trembling hands and with tears running down my face, I begged him to please make sure the officers were careful. "Sergeant, we just put our house on the market to relocate. Now I need to sell it more than ever before. Please ask them to be careful."

The sergeant returned shortly after exiting the room with my house key. "Do you have anyone you can call? Do you have any family or friends you can stay with?" the sergeant asked as he handed me another tissue. "The officers will be searching your house for hours, and I don't think it's a good idea for you to be alone."

People and places began whirling through my mind, and then I answered, "There are our boating friends, but I'm too humiliated to tell any of them. I have friends from work, but no, I could never face them now!" My chest felt like an elephant was sitting on it. I tried to think of someone with whom I would feel safe, but my thinking of someone was followed by an overwhelming sense of embarrassment and shame at the mere thought that I was actually married to a man who was capable to doing such defiling, destructive, horrendous things.

Then, out of the blue, it hit me. "My dad! I want my daddy!" I cried. "He was the one who gave me pep talks when I was a single mother. Yes, he's the only one I want right now. But he lives hours from here."

"Then let me call him right now," the sergeant said and then asked for my father's name and telephone number. He went around the corner to make the call, and tears poured down my face as I thought about Emily and the pain she must have endured. I was so grateful her nightmare had ended, but *six years!* What could be more horrible for my child? How could this have happened without my knowing it? How did she survive? Oh, how I wished she could have told me! I knew Emily knew how much I loved her—I would have done anything for her. Thoughts were spinning out of control. I could never hurt anything, but just the thought of somebody selfishly and purposely hurting one of my children caused me to recognize that I was capable of almost anything. If I had found out on my own, I might have even tried to use one of Lawrence's own weapons on him and ended up at the wrong end of the barrel—and I could have either ended up dead or in prison! Then what would have happened to my children? Both rage and helplessness consumed me as tears continued streaming down my cheeks.

The sergeant walked back into the room and informed me, "I just got off the telephone with your father. He and your stepmother are on their way. They should be arriving a little after ten o'clock tonight." He smiled as he went on to say, "As it turns out, I knew your father when I worked under his jurisdiction during the riots. Our department had sent a number of men to assist, and I went with them. As a battalion chief, your father had over three hundred men assigned to him, and I was one of them."

I was happy the call went well, but all I could hear was that they were on their way, and the news felt like a warm blanket had just been wrapped around me after I had been rescued from a freezing river. I was paralyzed by fear, sickened for my daughter, worried about my son, and completely confused about how it all could have happened and where to go on from here. I definitely needed the safe love and support of my father and stepmother, much more than I could ever express.

After declining the sergeant's offer for water or coffee, he sat down and said, "Wendy, we are aware that you didn't know what was going on." I looked up in surprise at his comment. "Your daughter was here for over thirteen hours last night, going into great detail as to how and when the abuse took place, as well as how it was hidden from you."

"Emily was here in your station last night? Is she still here or in town? Can I see her?"

"No, once we were done gathering all the information, your ex-husband received approval from Child Protective Services to take your children a few hours away, where they are staying with a close friend of his," he replied. "But as it turns out, they had called your father earlier to give him a heads-up. Your father had his bags packed, ready to leave, when I called him. He wasn't allowed to tell you anything, as we didn't know how you would react when you found out. We could not risk jeopardizing the arrest, but most important, your daughter was afraid for your life. She was always told and was convinced that you would kill yourself if you ever found out."

"You mean Emily was wearing the weight of my life on her shoulders all the time Lawrence was abusing her?" I screamed. Uncontrollable sobbing poured out as my entire body went limp. I could hardly hold myself up in my chair as I thought of what Emily had gone through. The pain was more than I could bear but not nearly as much as what Emily had endured.

I realized that recent events had placed an incredible burden on my daughter—a burden that I thought I had been carrying by myself. Lawrence had become more interested in spending time with a group of people who would party and drink to excess. Three weeks ago, on a boating weekend with some of these people, including Branton, who had been arrested in this crime, it became impossible to ignore the effects their company had on my husband. Lawrence was not acting like himself. He was drinking more and flirting with other women. The night we returned from the trip, I said to him, "I don't think I fit into your world anymore, and I don't want to."

Lawrence became enraged and threw the television remote across the bedroom at the wall. I was frightened by his outburst, but I stayed firm as I backed myself up against the dresser, holding my ground in response to his anger. He eventually broke down crying, kneeling by the side of the bed and begging my forgiveness. I was so confused by his behavior; I had to leave the room, so I decided to take a shower. As soon as the warm water hit my skin, I burst out crying and slid down the inside of the shower wall and onto the floor. I took my razor and started to knick at my wrist with it, seeing the small amount of blood go down the drain. "I feel like I'm going crazy!" I wailed. "I can't take this anymore!"

Lawrence heard the commotion and came into the bathroom. After seeing the situation, he called Emily into the bathroom to help me out of the shower and bandage my wrist. No wonder Emily thought I wouldn't be able to help her escape from his torment! In hindsight, I realized that Lawrence's calling Emily in the bathroom at that moment was a deliberate move—a way to validate the lies he had told her about what would happen to me if she told me about him.

The next morning, we learned the children's grandfather had passed away. I reapplied the bandages on my wrists, wearing a long-sleeved shirt to cover the evidence, and drove the kids to their grandmother's house, several hours away.

With over four hours still to go before my father and stepmother would arrive, I tried to collect myself and slowly began asking the sergeant questions.

He leaned forward in his chair and explained. "After thirteen hours of gathering evidence from your daughter, we recorded a call that she made to your husband at about ten thirty last night. Lawrence profusely admitted his guilt on the telephone call with Emily. We had given her a script of comments and questions to ask. She had told us exactly how he would answer them, and she was right. He answered the way she said he would answer, almost word for word."

"Like what kind of questions?" I asked.

"Well, for one thing, she told him she wanted him to stop, and he promised her a dog. Just exactly what she told us he would say."

"A dog?" I replied.

"Yes," the sergeant went on, "it seems Lawrence frequently told Emily he was going to get her a dog. Abusive and manipulative actions are merely a way of continuing to inflict power and control, usually preempted and followed by repeated threats and promises. It's what predators do—they use force, fear, shame, lies, and guilt."

"Sergeant, did my daughter ever explain what gave her the courage to finally tell?" I asked.

"Well," he said, "as you may know, your children and their father stopped in Texas after Oklahoma, so Emily could visit her girlfriend. It was there that your daughter ended up telling her girlfriend Ashley. She's a good friend!" he exclaimed. "After Emily opened up, Ashley was able to talk your daughter into sharing the truth with her mother. At that point, both Ashley and her mother were able to convince your daughter to tell her father. Mitch immediately got in the car and drove your children to the police department. The officers redirected him to us, as the most recent crimes were committed in our jurisdiction. As I mentioned, we had Emily here for over thirteen hours yesterday. This is an extremely delicate case because of your husband's history and work with law enforcement. We had to be surer than sure before initiating an arrest. There could be no doubt."

"So you have the men in custody now?" I asked, assuming the evidence was rock solid.

"They were each brought in within minutes of your own arrival," he replied. "We sent a van with four of our men to the academy this morning to pick Lawrence up. It was a very sensitive matter. We had to arrest him in the weapons unit itself, knowing full well he had an entire array of accessible weapons at his disposal, if he chose to use them."

The more the sergeant spoke, the more I was convinced that this nightmare was really happening. It was not a dream; it was real. With one phone call, everything I had ever hoped for and wanted was destroyed forever.

Chapter 2

Swept Away

As I sat in the sergeant's office, knowing full well it would be another four hours before my father and stepmother's arrival, flashbacks of the day before spiraled through my mind.

I mumbled my thoughts out loud, as if the sergeant wasn't even there. "It was about one o'clock in the afternoon yesterday, when Lawrence and my girlfriend Melissa drove off in their separate vehicles, heading a few hours north. Melissa had just come down for the weekend. She was so excited that we were moving back to her area, and she wanted to help me get the house ready to show. Funny thing is, one of the last things I asked Lawrence before he drove away was if the next house we bought could have an oval tub, like in our previous house. He looked at me and said, 'We'll see.'"

My eyes were fixed on a piece of carpet fiber coming up from the floor as I continued. "A couple of hours later, I was doing things around the house when suddenly an overwhelming sense of fear and doom hit me. It felt similar to what I had experienced before, only this time it was worse than anything previously. It was crushing me from the inside out. I feared that something was wrong, and thoughts of my children kept flashing through my mind. Most especially, thoughts of Christopher kept invading my heart until an uncontainable sickening sadness overcame me. The anxious thoughts flooded my heart and head, to the point that tears welled in my eyes. I knew my children had one more week to go on their trip, but somehow I felt a very strong urge to find them. So in an attempt to decrease my anxiety and assure myself they were all right, I picked up the telephone and began calling around."

The sergeant was silent and let me continue to explain. "I tried to track down my children by the route they were taking. I called their grandmother in Oklahoma and then Emily's friend in Texas. I tracked down Mitch's friends in Las Vegas but to no avail; I couldn't find my children. I felt so helpless. Then I had a thought—Mitch is always in contact with his best friend, William. I picked up the telephone in one last attempt, but nobody knew where my children were."

I looked up at the sergeant, staring at his eyes, as if trying to verify the thought that had just hit me. "That feeling I had, just like before—it was telling me that something really was wrong! It wasn't paranoia! I wasn't going crazy! My children were right here, two miles from home, when I was calling all over the country for them. No wonder I felt such a sad and painful yearning for them."

My mind continued to process the events that had taken place over the past twenty-four hours. I remembered that I'd gone to bed feeling very troubled the previous night. I was restless and had tossed and turned for over an hour. I had barely gotten to sleep when I was awakened by the telephone ringing at about eleven o'clock—it was Lawrence.

He said he had arrived safely at his daughter's house and was getting ready to go to bed. The tone of his voice sounded uneasy, and I asked him if he was all right. He didn't seem like himself; he sounded distressed, but every time I tried to ask him about it, he turned the conversation to me. Lawrence said he was worried about me and wanted to know if I was okay. I assured him I was fine but that his call had woke me up. That seemed to satisfy him—until about seven o'clock the next morning, when he called again to see how I was doing.

"I am good," I said. "Just getting ready for work. It won't be much longer and I'll be up there!" We hung up after wishing each other a good day at work.

Another realization struck me. "Sergeant, did you tell me that you had Emily call Lawrence last night at about ten thirty?"

"That's correct," the sergeant answered.

"Lawrence called me at eleven o'clock. That must have been right after he hung up with Emily."

"Lawrence was probably checking things out. He knew you were at home and that your daughter was out of town, but perhaps he felt like something was up. He most likely wanted to make sure you didn't know about the call," the sergeant responded.

"The last time I spoke to Lawrence was at eleven this morning," I said. "He called me at work. He said all the other officers had been called up to a meeting in the administration building but that he hadn't been invited. Lawrence told me he was using the downtime to give me a call, to see if I was okay."

"That was right after our men and van arrived at the academy," the sergeant replied, "They had to strategically plan with the academy staff just how the arrest would take place without anyone getting hurt."

As I put the pieces together in my mind, it all began to make sense—Lawrence's probing questions and calls, the unsettled feeling in my gut—yet nothing made sense. Emily's childhood had been stolen from her, and my life as I knew it was now over.

I still had hours before my parents would arrive. The sergeant walked in and out of his office throughout those remaining hours. I could tell he was checking on me, but it was obvious he had much more going on. More specifically, he was working on the other end of the equation—the arrested ones. I sat there in shock, my head spinning, my heart aching, with visions of the children and my entire life rolling by. The sensation reminded me of a time when I was eight years old. I had been knocked over backward by a massive wave at the beach. The water was turbulent, and it thrust me around on the sand. No matter how hard I tried to reach the surface with each of my limbs, I couldn't. The wave finally receded, allowing a much needed breathe and the ability to right myself, but only after watching my entire life flash before my eyes, as if it were about to end.

It was close to ten o'clock when the sergeant came back into the room to sit down. He had a compassionate look on his face as he observed my stricken expression. "Sergeant," I said, "Lawrence didn't want my children to go on this trip with their father. We didn't have many disagreements, but this was one of them. He was so angry about it that he punched a hole in our kitchen wall when I insisted they were going."

Feeling dazed, my eyes drifted to the floor as I continued to sort out the numerous memories that flooded my mind. I tried desperately to analyze each one as it came to me. I faintly heard the sergeant's phone ring, and then he excused himself. A few minutes later, I could hear multiple footsteps coming toward the office door. As I looked up, there were my father and stepmother. With newfound energy, I jumped from my chair and grabbed them both. With tears running down my face, and all shame and embarrassment set aside for the moment, I held onto them for what seemed like an eternity. I wouldn't and couldn't let go.

Eventually, the sergeant spoke up to regain our attention. He explained it would be hours before we would be allowed back into my home. And with no other place to go at ten thirty at night, we ended up in a twenty-four-hour restaurant, just a few blocks from the police station. Sadness overwhelmed the conversation, and although my stepmother ordered me soup, I couldn't put a thing in my mouth. "Try hot tea," she suggested, but my head was spinning with confusion, and it was apparent I was not the only one in shock.

With my father's career in the fire department and Lawrence's career in law enforcement, they had developed a sense of solidarity over the years and a deep respect for each other. As a matter of fact, my father said he was having a hard time believing what he had been told, and when he was first informed about the abuse, he initially insisted that Mitch or Emily must have made it up. But now that the arrest had taken place and all the evidence backed it up, he was beginning to accept it as well. The image of his wonderful son-in-law had been shattered. "Lawrence always came off as such a great guy. He was so convincing," my father said.

"Yes, he sure had all of us fooled, didn't he?" That was all I could mutter in response.

Around one in the morning, my father began calling the police station every half hour or so to find out the status on the house search. Finally, a little after two thirty in the morning, they said we could come back to the station and pick up my house key. I absolutely hated the thought of walking back into that station. It wasn't because of the officers; they had been kind and sympathetic. It was because I knew the men who had hurt Emily so horribly with their heinous acts were somewhere close by, and the very thought of being in the same building sent chills up and down my spine.

As we entered the police station, we were directed to the back of the building, where we would find the men who had done the investigation. They had just returned to the station and were still suited up in their search gear. "The investigators tried to be careful, ma'am," the officer said. He handed me my house key and asked for my signature on a multiple-page form that listed all the evidence they had confiscated. Then he said, "We've searched a lot of homes, ma'am, but yours was by far the cleanest we've ever been in. It helped make the search go more quickly. Your home should still look presentable. The officers tried to keep things tidy."

I nodded, thanked him, and then murmured, "We just put our home on the market."

I knew the officer was trying to be pleasant during such a difficult situation, but I could only think, *Home? What home? My husband's gone, and every fond memory I've ever had of him is destroyed. My children are gone, and my daughter's been completely robbed of her childhood. Home no longer exists.* My entire life had just been swept away.

Chapter 3

The Light Bulb

It was after three in the morning before my parents and I were allowed to enter my home. As I led the way through the garage entrance and into the house, I turned on every light in my path until the entire house was lit up. I was struck with the eeriest feeling as I walked from room to room. Everything was the same, only slightly different. The carpet indentations told me that every piece of furniture in the house had been moved and then put back in almost the original position. Wiring and computer cords had been labeled with tape to ensure they were properly reconnected. Even the attic opening was sitting a little differently than before, showing that it had been altered as well. It was quickly apparent that nothing had gone unturned. Everything had been looked under, over, in, and around. Once again, the reality of what had happened slapped me boldly in the face.

I felt violated in my own home—not so much because of the police and their search but because of the man I had believed in, relied on, and entrusted with the most precious thing in the world to me, my children. This man's evil acts, his lies, and all the deceit he represented had destroyed Emily's childhood and every good thing he had ever meant to me.

As I looked from room to room, all I could think of was the pain and suffering that my daughter had gone through. I leaned against the doorframe that led into Emily's bedroom and began to sob uncontrollably.

"It's almost four in the morning. You need to get some sleep," my stepmother said. Both she and my father gently guided me toward the master bedroom. Without speaking, I slowly and painfully went into the bedroom.

As I entered the room, my feet carried me forward until I found myself gazing into the walk-in closet. I stopped inside the doorframe and slowly scanned up and down and across the double layer of neatly organized clothes hanging along his side of the closet—his shirts, his pants, and, on the floor, his boots. A piercing ache shot through my heart, and I clutched my chest in a futile attempt to stop it. I had to turn away. As I looked up at the light bulb in the ceiling, the most profound thought hit me: *I've been putting all my faith and trust in a man! I should have been putting it in God!*

As I staggered toward the bed, my thoughts began spilling out aloud. "I've never met a perfect person. He's human; he's not perfect. Why was I putting all my faith and trust in him? Of course Lawrence was going to let me down. Of course it was too good to be true." Flashes of prior conversations flew through my mind as I recalled how many times a week I heard Lawrence tell me how much he loved me, how he'd always be there for me, how I'd never find anybody else who would love me as much as he did, and most especially, how faithful he was to me. With every thought came a deeper pain, a dagger through my heart and down toward my stomach.

Still wearing my work clothes and shoes, I flopped down across my bed. All I could do was lie there, staring aimlessly at the ceiling. My head was spinning. I was overwhelmed and exhausted, yet in so much shock I could not close my eyes. Instead, I lay there in a daze while thoughts of my entire life went whizzing by—one by one, event after event—bringing me all the way up to this moment in time. It was like a dreadful movie with the worst of endings playing on a continuous loop in my mind.

"But he was supposed to be my Mr. Wonderful!" I cried out in anguish. I recalled how Lawrence had come into my life. Mitch had left when Emily was four and Christopher was just turning three years old. I had been a single mother for three years before marrying my Mr. Wonderful (that is what I called him and how I introduced him). I had been swept away by his charm, grace, and undivided attention. Lawrence continuously reminded me of how beautiful he thought I was. He represented everything I thought I ever wanted. A day didn't go by when he didn't grab my arm or put my hand in his as we walked. My new life with him was like a waltz— graceful, engaging, captivating, joyful, and full of surprise. And I thought it was a love affair that would never end. Lawrence was handsome, strong, dependable, reliable, fun, and exciting ... that is, until the past six months or so. That's when I began noticing some considerable changes in him. He wasn't as thoughtful, he became extremely self-focused, and his desire for pornography escalated. It was as if a beast had gotten hold of him and wouldn't let go. He began hanging out with his newfound friend Branton more often, and his desire to do things with our old friends diminished.

But wait, I thought, *this abuse was going on for six years, not six months!* That meant Lawrence had fooled me for six of our seven and a half years of marriage. It wasn't until he involved his new friend Branton that he began acting differently. It wasn't until the commingling of their crimes that his core character flaws became increasingly apparent.

As I considered the craziness I had experienced over the past six months—the gut-wrenching anxiety and the unexplainable unsettledness—I flashed back to a moment in time that is now ingrained in my mind forever. It was a particular day when I was driving home from work and had just passed my counselor's office. I recalled the multiple visits when Mr. Ellis and I were unable to get to the root of my unrest. As I continued down the road, my eyes began to well up with tears as I realized how helpless I felt—and then the floodgates opened, and I cried so profusely that I had to pull the car over to the side of the road. I could not continue driving. My tears were like rain. With every ounce of strength in me, I screamed at the top of my lungs, *"Help me, God!"*

I had no idea what caused me to yell out to God. I had not included or recognized God in my life since I was a teen. Eighteen years earlier, when I was raped and beaten by a music minister's son, I had vowed never to walk into another church again for as long as I lived. But suddenly, in desperation, I cried out to the only thing I thought could be bigger than the agony I was going through.

As I continued staring at the textured ceiling in my bedroom, it dawned on me—could everything happening now be God's answer to my cry? I started to remember the events which transpired shortly after I'd called out to God.

It was right after I cried out to God for help that Lawrence was offered a job at the academy. Then Emily and Christopher's grandfather passed away and Emily was able to visit Ashley in Texas, which somehow triggered her ability to tell what was going on. My mind continued connecting the many dots and events which had fallen into place.

If there is a God, I thought, *then God must have heard me, and God must be answering my cry for help now.* It was the only explanation that could end a six-year nightmare for Emily so abruptly and explain the gut-wrenching pain I had been experiencing. As I thought more about it, I never once closed my eyes that night and eventually became aware that rays of sunlight were making their way across the floor, shining through the French doors. It was morning, and somehow I had made it through the worst night of my life. I could hear my father and stepmother walking down the hall toward the kitchen. I wanted to get up, but I couldn't move a muscle, so there I lay for another hour or so.

It was about nine o'clock on Tuesday, July 2, when the telephone rang—but the ringing stopped before I could reach it. I faintly heard my father's voice say hello—he had answered the telephone in the kitchen. Numb and lethargic, I forced myself off the bed, and when I opened the bedroom door, I heard my father say, "Just a minute; I think I hear her coming." My steps were slow and tiny as I mustered up the will to make my way down the hall and into the kitchen. My father covered the mouthpiece on the phone and then looked up at me and said, "It's your realtor. He has an offer on the house. He said the buyers want to pay cash and close in two weeks."

I stood there in shock, staring at my father. "I don't know what to do!"

My father got back on the telephone. "Can we call you back?" he asked the realtor. "Wendy just got up, and we need to talk about it for a few minutes." My father ended the call nicely and then got up to hold me tightly. He could see the confusion and distress on my face. It was quickly apparent to him that I had not slept one bit. The tears and shock had washed my face as white as a ghost, and the dark circles around my eyes were hollow and sunken.

"Why don't you go take a shower," my father said. "Just give it some thought, and then we can call the realtor back."

What he said made perfect sense, and I agreed to take a shower in an attempt to revive myself. I took a change of clothes into my bathroom but stopped abruptly and turned back, heading to the children's bathroom instead. Somehow, I felt safer and closer to my children by using their bathroom. As I set my clothes on the counter and turned the water on, I could think only of how confused I was. I didn't know what to do!

As the warm water from the shower streamed down my face, I began to sob again. Questions plagued me. *Do I stay, or do I go? We already have a home here, and I have a job. And where would we go if we left? But wait—I don't know if I can afford this place on my own! Oh, what do I do?* My thoughts overwhelmed me once again, and I cried out in agony, *"God! What do I do?"*

Suddenly, the words to a country song by Martina McBride rang loudly through my head, as if it was electronically piped into the shower. "It's Independence Day!" The title words and tune kept repeating in my mind, over and over again. *Where did that come from?* I turned my face toward heaven and cried out, "Is that you, God? Is that you? Are you answering me?"

Unexpectedly, a comfort like nothing I had ever felt before consumed me from the inside out. The sensation was instantaneous and like warm honey; it ran through my body from the top of my head to the bottoms of my feet. A peace entered me, if only for a moment, and I knew it was God. I don't know how I knew, exactly, but I definitely knew. The realization consumed me. It was the first time I had ever experienced anything like that. I knew God was talking to me. Even more so, he was talking to me in a language I could understand.

"It's you, God! It's you!" I exclaimed in amazement. "I know it's you. You're telling me what to do. It's time to be free! It's time to get out of here! It's Independence Day!" I quickly finished my shower, dried off, and got dressed. I could hardly wait to tell my father what I was going to do. I ran back into the kitchen, calling out, "I am supposed to sell the house! I don't know where I'm going, and I don't know where I'll work, but let's get the realtor on the phone right now!"

My father and I decided not to mention our nightmare to the realtor. When my father called him back, he said he was extremely excited to have found a buyer so soon; he hadn't even shown the property yet. "The funny thing is," the realtor said, "the people making the offer said they saw the house on Saturday. It must have been right after I put the FOR SALE sign up in the yard. They said the owners showed them the home."

When my father repeated what the realtor had said, I realized that so much had happened over the past seventeen hours that I was having a hard time remembering anything from three days earlier. I tried to recall the events from Saturday.

"It was Melissa!" I said. "Melissa was here on Saturday. She was helping me get the house ready to sell. We were standing at the kitchen sink, and she saw a car drive up. The people got out of their car to grab a flyer from the box on the FOR SALE sign, but we hadn't put them out yet. Melissa grabbed a flyer off the counter and ran out to them before they drove away. She told them to come in and take a look since they were already here. I looked up at my father. "Dad, I just remembered—I was running through the house, turning all the lights on and opening the blinds as she walked them to our entrance."

Once again I wondered, *Could it be that God is here and is continuing to answer my cry for help? Could it be that he really heard me and is responding? Could it be that these events—from Emily's nightmare ending to finding a buyer for the house—are all part of his answer and plan?*

Cash and close in two weeks? That was unheard of these days. And Melissa—look how she showed up in my life again just a few weeks earlier, after I'd lost contact with her for over three years. She had come into town on business and run into our mutual boating friends at lunch. They gave her my number, and she called. Melissa was here just in time to help. She was the one who ran with a flyer for the house hunters—the ones making an offer.

The "coincidences" were adding up. There was a definite chain of events, each incident colliding together at this particular moment in time—and they began the moment I had cried out to God for help. It was evident, beyond any doubt, that there was more to this than what I could see or comprehend. It was as if there was a Master Conductor, watching from above, who was orchestrating the entire thing.

> *"Call on me when you are in trouble,*
> *and I will rescue you."*
> —Psalm 50:15 (NLT)

Chapter 4

Facing the World

My stepmother tried to coax me into eating some breakfast, but I just couldn't do it. My stomach was tied in knots. Bouts of fear, anxiety, and humiliation rushed through me as I thought about everyone at work finding out what had happened. The majority of the staff knew Lawrence and had watched him take me to lunch a couple of times a week since the day I began working there.

Over time and with numerous hours of hard work, I had built a wonderful relationship with the staff in both the hospice and home health care divisions of the medical center. Suddenly, I blurted out to my parents, "I must tell the people at my workplace what has happened before they find out another way!" This was something I knew I needed to do. I just didn't know how I was going to do it.

Glancing at the clock and the calendar below it, I realized I had a counselor's appointment in less than a half hour. I had forgotten all about it. The previous plan was that after my appointment, I would head to the train station, but now, I would go to my workplace instead. I still needed to go to my counseling appointment first. I wanted to tell Mr. Ellis that I was not going crazy after all and there was a reason for all the

27

gut-wrenching and horrible feelings I had been experiencing. I informed my parents of my plan and then grabbed my purse and headed out the door.

As Mr. Ellis entered the waiting room from his private office door, he took a step back in surprise when he first saw me. My sunken, bloodshot eyes might have frightened him a bit. He glanced around the empty room as he walked toward me. "Wendy, are you okay? Is everything all right?"

I slowly got up from my chair and, without a word, walked into his office. Tears began to flow again, and I could barely speak the words. "I was not going crazy! My gut knew something was wrong. I could not see it, but my body and soul knew it was there!"

Then I proceeded to tell him the nightmare that had transpired over the past eighteen hours.

Mr. Ellis's eyes welled up with tears, and he quickly pulled a tissue from a box on the table and patted his eyes. It appeared the news had mortified him as well. We both recalled the number of times Lawrence had joined our prior sessions.

"He tricked us all," I said, staring directly at his face. "Nobody can believe it. But it all makes sense now, doesn't it, Mr. Ellis?"

My appointment ended with a sorrowful good-bye. With tears in my eyes, I got back in my car and headed down the street toward my workplace. As I pulled up near the entrance, I froze in my car. I couldn't seem to get my body to move, and it took every ounce of courage to finally open the car door. Some of the staff seemed surprised to see me walk in.

"I thought you were going on vacation. What are you doing here?" one of them said.

I forced myself to keep walking down the hall and right into my boss's office. Stephen looked up and then quickly jumped out of his chair when he saw the look on my face.

"Is everything okay?" Stephen asked me.

"I have something that's very difficult to say. I need to tell everyone at once. Can we have all the available staff come into your office as well?"

"Sure," Stephen said. He darted outside his office and began rounding up all the office and field staff who were in the hospice portion of the building. As I sat there in his office, my head lowered, fiddling with the strap of my purse, I could see a number of feet enter the room.

"I think we are all here," Stephen said in a tender voice.

I dreaded looking up, but the admiration I held for each one of them gave me the courage to raise my head in spite of my fear. There before me stood the people I had learned to love and respect—the medical director, the nuns, the chaplain, one of our social workers, the nursing director, and a number of other nurses and aides on staff.

"I need to tell you this before you find out from another source and before it hits the news or something ..." Tears began pouring down my face, and I couldn't get another word out of my mouth.

They stood there, patiently waiting, as I tried to collect myself. Through bouts of uncontrollable weeping, I managed to explain the story of the disaster. *They are used to dealing with loss*, I thought as they huddled around me, trying to provide comfort. But the more I tried to explain, the less I was able to say. Just hearing myself talk to them threw me into another abrasive wave of shock. I froze, dropped my head, and sobbed uncontrollably.

I had managed to drive myself there, but I was in no shape to drive myself home. One of the nurses quickly asked for my physician's name. She was able to get him on the telephone and then took off in a hurry, saying she was picking up some medication the doctor had ordered for me. Eventually, the nurse returned, and I was able to calm down. Robert, one of the social workers, said he would drive me home and have Sister Margaret, one of the nuns, follow in my car. *I couldn't work for a more compassionate group of people*, I thought. Perhaps God knew I'd need them and their support as well.

As Robert drove me home, I shared with him the unsettled feeling I'd been experiencing for months and how I finally cried out to God in desperation. He said he got goose bumps when I told him all the events that had transpired since I asked for God's help, including the offer on the house earlier that same day. Robert agreed that it sounded like divine intervention.

"But I didn't do anything to deserve it," I said in a puzzled tone. "All I did was cry out for help to a God I had shunned for eighteen years."

As we pulled up to my home, I saw my mother standing next to my father and stepmother in the driveway. Panic struck me.

"*No!* I don't want her here!" I shrieked. Robert seemed surprised at my reaction, especially when I turned my face away from the house to avoid looking at her. He slowly parked the car and waved to Sister Margaret, signaling that she should park in front of him. I couldn't move from my seat. Robert got out of the car and walked around to open my door, reaching in to help me out. Reluctantly, I raised my hand for his assistance.

As my coworkers walked along beside me up the driveway from the street, I looked at my mother and said, "What are you doing here? Go away!"

In an attempt to defuse the awkwardness, Robert reached out his hand toward my father and introduced himself, going on to explain the emotional breakdown I had experienced at the office and why they had decided to drive me home.

After giving me a hug and confirming that I was in good hands, Robert and Sister Margaret said good-bye. I turned once again to my mother and said, "I don't want you here. I want you to leave."

A choice my mother made over seven years earlier had hurt me deeply. She later requested forgiveness, but I wouldn't give it. Instead I kept my distance and was only cordial when necessary at family functions. I felt she had been wrong, and I didn't want her to see me now as a failure myself.

My father explained that Mitch had called my mother first. She had checked into a hotel yesterday and was waiting for a phone call to say that I'd been told. My mother tried to express her love and concern, but I didn't want to hear it and quickly turned my back to her.

"Wendy," my father said, "while you were gone, we received a call from Mitch. He and the children are staying with William, his attorney friend, right now, a few hours north of here."

"How are Emily and Christopher?" I asked quickly. "How are they doing? Did you talk to them?" I wasn't ready for the next wave to hit, but it did anyway.

"I am afraid Mitch is taking you to court. He wants full custody of the children," my dad said.

"What?" I exclaimed. "How can he have custody? He doesn't even have his own place to live! He hasn't even been able to hold down a job!"

"Well, you need to explain that fact to the judge," my father answered, "because your court date is scheduled for tomorrow afternoon at one o'clock. You'll have to leave early since the courthouse is a few hours north of here."

I stumbled in shock toward the house. "No! Don't take my children away too!" I bellowed. Fear raced through me, paralyzing me once again. As my head spun, I tried putting myself in Mitch's shoes. *He just wants to know the children will be safe. It's not like he can take care of them. He can barely afford to take care of himself,* I thought. I stopped walking and quickly turned around to ask my parents, "Can he really take them away from me?"

"I don't know," my father answered. "Let me get my attorney on the telephone."

My father's attorney was located over five hundred miles away from where the custody hearing would take place. The attorney said he would not be able to represent me in the hearing the next day but that he could help me out in another way. He offered to gather all the information required and then fax to me the documents needed to file for divorce.

"It's too late to make it to the courthouse today," the attorney explained, "but you could file for divorce first thing in the morning, before you leave town for the custody hearing." He explained that if I could file for divorce when the courthouse opened and bring copies of the filing with me, it would help support my intent and confirm that I had absolutely no intention of ever allowing Lawrence near my children again.

After speaking with the attorney, I pulled out our address book to get the number of some friends, a married couple who both practiced law in the city where the courthouse was located. They were Lawrence's friends, but I needed to call someone. I had to find an attorney who would represent me in court the next day, or I might lose the case and then my children.

These friends were shocked when I told them what had happened. They couldn't believe that their good friend, someone they'd known for years, had actually done what he did. They felt awkward yet also inclined to help. They made a few calls and then called me back with a referral to another attorney, Ms. Miller, a woman who specialized in family law.

When I called Ms. Miller, she agreed to take the case and set up an appointment for the next morning. She explained, "After you file your divorce papers with the county courthouse, I want you to call me by 9:00 a.m. We will discuss your case on the phone while you are driving to the hearing. I will then meet you at the courthouse a little before 1:00 p.m. The cost will be $1,300 for me to represent you tomorrow."

"Whatever it takes," I replied. "I just want my children back."

My mother pulled money from her wallet, offering to help out with the legal fees. Then she got on the telephone and found a local business where we could receive a faxed document. We would be able to have the completed divorce documents sent there. I appreciated my mother's help, but I didn't want to admit it. My attention had been taken off her and was focused toward the most important thing in the world to me—my children and getting them back safely in my arms.

In the midst of all this, my father and stepmother informed me they were going home that afternoon. "Your mother is here now, and we have an appointment tomorrow that we really should not miss," my father said. "Your mother has agreed to stay with you for as long as you need, and she has also offered to drive you to the courthouse and then up to the hearing in the morning."

My heart sank. *No,* I thought, *I don't want to be left alone here with my mother.*

I nervously hugged my father and stepmother good-bye. I couldn't stop thanking them for being there for me, and now I didn't want them to leave. They had just helped me through the worst twenty-four hours of my life, and it didn't look like the next twenty-four hours were going to be any easier. Once again, my mother expressed her love and concern for me, but all I could do was drop my head in despair and shame.

Within four and a half hours of my father's forewarning me, I was going to court regarding the custody of my children, I had the completed documents in hand and was ready to file for divorce. I would be required to take the documents inside the courthouse myself and file them with the county clerk. The county courthouse opened at 8:00 a.m., and I had to be right there when the doors opened. We figured I only had a half hour to complete the filing process and then get on the road to drive the two hundred miles to the courthouse, or I would never make it in time for the hearing.

It was getting late, and my mother could see the fatigue taking hold of me. She tried to get me to eat something, but I still wasn't hungry. After taking a few sips of water, I excused myself to my bedroom. I had been up for two days straight without any sleep and my body was completely worn out. I was dreadfully overwhelmed with fear and anxiety as I realized that everything important to me had been ripped away, and now I had a fight on my hands to regain the one thing that meant everything—my children.

Chapter 5

Forgiveness

I was completely exhausted as I climbed into bed, yet my mind kept spinning and wouldn't shut down. I tossed and turned, recalling the events which had transpired seven years earlier with my mother and the reasons I'd decided to disconnect from her. I believed her decision was wrong, and no matter how nice she was acting toward me, I did not want to forgive her, as I felt justified in holding on to my anger.

The clock ticked away as I lay awake. All of a sudden, as if a light bulb had just been turned on in my head, I realized that if God could love and help me while I was broken and making my own wrong choices, then indeed I could forgive my mother for making a bad choice too.

I grew up thinking that if I forgave someone, it was like condoning his or her actions, sort of the "forgive and forget" philosophy. But I was beginning to see the truth in that I could forgive the person, yet still disagree with his or her actions— just as I was sure God was not always pleased with my choices but chose to love me anyway.

I decided I was going to forgive my mother and be kind to her, even if I didn't agree with her. And the fact that she was demonstrating a humble attitude helped lessen the pain of allowing her back into my life. My brain began to settle down, and with that last thought, I slowly drifted off to sleep for the first time in over forty-two hours.

It was a little before seven the next morning when we headed out the front door, first to the local courthouse downtown and then north to the hearing. Thoughts of my children and the anticipation of being able to see them later that day brought comfort to my aching heart. I wanted to wrap my arms around them and never let go. I wanted to tell them how sorry I was and ask them for their forgiveness. I wanted to hold my little girl and tell her how grateful and proud I was that she had the courage to tell someone.

As I headed toward my mother's car, I almost tripped over the morning paper on the walkway. I glanced at it—and there it was, the ugly truth, staring me in the face once again. Our story had hit the news. The newspaper's blazing headline announced the arrest of the two men charged with the abuse of my daughter. Terror shot up and down my spine as I realized the word was out. Overwhelming feelings of loss and public humiliation swallowed me up; I could hardly move or breathe. It was like being fastened to a sinking ship that was taking me down with it, and there was nothing I could do to break loose. How could I have been married to a man who did such terrible things? *There will be no more hiding or holding back*, I thought. The paper just let the entire world know of our tragedy.

My hands began to shake as I picked up the paper. I attempted to read the article to my mother as she drove down the road, but my voice quivered and tears flowed down my face. The article mentioned that the primary suspect's charges were equal to a ninety-eight-year sentence. Over and over again, the truth of what we were facing viciously turned me upside down and inside out.

I had heard many stories throughout the years—different children and girls kidnapped and held prisoner by an abusive, controlling predator, sometimes even losing their lives in the end. But I always thought my children and I would be safe because I had married a man who represented the law and authority. Lawrence was supposed to be the one who rescued, not the one from whom my daughter needed to be rescued.

Emily had been held a prisoner too. She had been subjected to ongoing mental, emotional, and physical abuse by a man's convoluted, evil, manipulative, and controlling ways. She didn't have to be kidnapped and taken to some unknown location; no, the abuse was concealed right in our midst. I could not help but wonder how many other children were being held prisoners in their own homes, in their own neighborhoods, or in their own communities.

The dreadful words from the newspaper article ran through my mind over and over as we continued to the courthouse. I wondered if I would ever be able to forgive myself for marrying this man. My choice ended up destroying my daughter's innocent childhood, robbing her of her joy, vivaciousness, safety, and trust; leaving fear, anger, resentment, mistrust, and a broken view on life in its place. This realization left me feeling helpless, regretful, and full of anger, but most of all, I was bursting with sorrow.

As we pulled up to the courthouse, my hands gripped the newspaper so tightly that my knuckles were white. It was now time to undo what little I could of the mistakes of the past. In reality, the husband I thought I had—the person I believed him to be—was gone; he'd never really existed at all. I had made some bad choices in my life, but marrying him and inviting him into my children's world was the worst possible mistake I ever could have made. If I had just known the truth about Lawrence, everything would have been different, and I never would have married him. The ramifications were immeasurably devastating. Now, my children were gone, and the only thing keeping me going was my great need to hold and protect them.

I was lightheaded from shock as I walked up the courthouse steps, but I was there before eight o'clock and one of the first in line to enter the building. With not only the court documents in hand but also the newspaper, my hands shook as I waited in line for the clerk. The clerk noticed the distressed look on my face as I stood at her window. I told myself I would show her the newspaper headline if she questioned me or if I ran into a problem. *Surely,* I thought, *if they know what I am up against, they will help.*

Eventually, after waiting in multiple lines, the court papers were processed, and I had certified copies in hand. I quickly headed back to the car and jumped in, crying out, "I have the copies we need. Let's go!"

Even though I had tried to hurry through the courthouse, it was already quarter to nine, and I was getting nervous. "Drive faster," I told my mother as we headed down the freeway. "We have to get there on time! My children's and my life together depends on it."

My mother sped up after I convinced her that if we were stopped by a law enforcement officer, I would shove the headline news in his face and ask for his assistance in getting us to the courthouse in time for the hearing. I sat there in the front seat with the newspaper across my lap, just daring an officer to try to stop me. I felt justified; after all, it was a law enforcement officer who had caused all this pain and need to rush in the first place.

It was nearly nine o'clock, which meant it was time to connect with Ms. Miller, the attorney representing my case. I called her on my cell phone, and she said she was taking notes. For the next three hours, we discussed the case and the history I had with the children's father.

Ms. Miller explained, "Because of what your daughter went through and because we do not know if Lawrence will be released on bail, it is very likely that the judge will grant custody to your ex-husband."

Fear raced through me like a lightning bolt. "Even if Lawrence did get out on bail, I would never let him near us!"

From the day Mitch left us, I had done everything I could possibly do to take care of and provide for my children. I was raised to take care of my own responsibilities and never even considered seeking outside assistance. The path that Mitch had chosen to walk, however, resembled that of a nomad, at least in my eyes. How could a judge put my two children into his hands?

Miraculously, we arrived at the courthouse by twelve thirty without ever being stopped or pulled over. Up the courthouse steps we ran. I will never forget the moment I saw Christopher and Emily again. I grabbed them tightly and held them as close as I possibly could as the tears ran down my face.

Then I turned to Mitch and his friend William, who was his representing attorney. "These children are the most important things in my life!" I said. "How could you try to take them away? You don't even have a home to live in. How can you take care of them? You don't have a job. You can't even afford child support. How are you going to pay for their food and their clothes?"

Mitch quickly explained that the officers at the police department had informed him they would not allow the children to be released into my custody because I was married to the perpetrator. Instead, the children would be placed in temporary foster care by Child Protective Services. Mitch thought this was an insane idea, so although he did not have legal custody, he demanded they be released into his care. The police only agreed to do so after he promised they would not be allowed near our home or their stepfather. His action was that of protection, not malice, as I had originally feared.

"And as it turns out," Mitch went on, "I don't have a job because every job I ever started either let me go or just fired me without any reason or warning within a week or two of being hired. Wendy, do you remember how the child support court order you obtained required me to provide you with a list of all the companies from which I sought employment each week? Do you know how many times I was hired and then let go? I used to ask them to explain why I was being let go, but they would always mumble some ridiculous reason that didn't make any sense!"

Mitch's face became more and more red with rage as he exclaimed, "Well, after the truth of what had been happening to our daughter came out, I remembered that the employer at one of those companies told me that right after I was hired, he received a call from a law enforcement officer, warning him that the man he had just hired—me—was a known child molester and pedophile! I thought my employer was lying to me, but now it all makes sense! You and your husband had the names of every company where I sought employment."

"What?" I exclaimed. "That is why you lost your job? I could never understand why you couldn't keep a job! It never made sense to me. I always remembered you being such a hard worker." Another streak of horror ran through my body as I realized who might have been the one to make that call, possibly the man who was guilty of such acts himself.

The very thought of such convoluted, evil manipulative ways caused me to cry out to Mitch, "Lawrence constantly pressured me to file a request for enforcement with the child support services court. It was his initial request that we be supplied with a copy of your weekly job searches. You were late and missed paying your child support obligations a few times. Lawrence said he refused to pay your part, that it was your responsibility to provide for your children, not his. That is why I even took on more work hours and then pushed to excel and be promoted. I did it so I could cover the financial obligations of what you didn't provide in child support." The depth of understanding struck me. "It appears we were both being sabotaged—your career constantly halted, creating a circumstance where you would never be able to have custody and where I would never be home. It looks like our daughter isn't the only victim in this horrible crime." Tears began running down my checks once again. "Thank God Emily had the courage to speak up," I cried as I grasped the children in my arms once again, unable to let them go.

I could tell Mitch was very angry, but he started to calm down as he saw the bigger picture and scope of the manipulation. Ms. Miller showed up, and a mediator was assigned to us in the hallway. After providing copies of the divorce papers I had just filed, a lengthy conversation, and my guaranteeing that I would never let the children anywhere near this horrific pedophile again, the mediator and attorneys took off down the hall to discuss the case with the judge.

It seemed like forever as we waited for the verdict. My conversation with Mitch became easier, and I thanked him profusely for taking the children, for listening to Emily when she had the courage to talk, and for taking them directly to the authorities who could do something about it. "It could not have been exposed in a better way," I told Mitch. "If I had found out on my own, I'd probably be dead right now, or at least behind bars ..."

At last, we saw the two attorneys walking toward us. "The children will be released back into your custody, Wendy," Ms. Miller explained, "but it was a close call. The judge needed to be persuaded of the children's safety. It is imperative that you do not let your husband near these children if he is released on bail."

"He is no longer my husband," I said flatly. "I have filed for divorce, and I would never let that man's evil sickness near my children again. I guarantee that with my life." As I glanced at Mitch, a look of concern yet relief crossed his face. I reached out and shook his hand, thanking him once again for caring for the children. I told him how sorry I was, as it looked like he had been a victim as well. My heart was filled with gratitude and compassion as I told him, "I hope your life can get back on track now. I truly wish you the very best." It was a sad yet sweet parting as I gathered the children in my arms, and we headed out of the courthouse.

Oh, God, I prayed silently, *I have my children back. Thank you so very much, God. I will do all that I can to make sure they are safe, but I have a feeling that I will not be able to do it without you. Please help us.*

Chapter 6

Running for Cover

The ride home seemed much quicker than the ride to the hearing. Anxieties had settled, and I was busy on the phone, informing loved ones that we were back together again and heading home safely. Once the calls were over, a million questions ran though my mind. I wanted so deeply to better understand what Emily had been going through, yet I didn't want to cause her any more pain. Slowly, little by little, she explained the things that had transpired until a picture of the events in my mind became more and more clear.

I could see the relief in Emily's eyes as she opened up to me and saw that I believed her. And there was relief from her biggest worry—that I wouldn't be able to handle it and would end my life, as she had always been told and had feared. Christopher, on the other hand, would speak only now and then, randomly interjecting a comment but usually just listening. I could see the pain and despair across his face as he learned the true reason for Lawrence's sending him to his friend's house to play after school each day. Christopher also had been let down in his own way; he had admired his stepfather, and now he was left with nothing but deep betrayal.

The pain was deep, and everything that had happened could be best described as far beyond horrible. Yet the realization that God was somehow involved in these current events and that he was apparently continuing to answer my cry for help gave me a new foundation to stand on—one which told me we were not alone and that someone bigger and stronger was now in charge.

The children were glad to be home. They had been living out of a suitcase for nearly three weeks as they'd traveled across the United States. We quickly unpacked their bags and then flopped down on the couch, happy to stretch out and take a breather. Emily snuggled up under my arm on the couch, and it felt so wonderful to have her close by my side. We looked at each other and tried to guess how long it had been since we had snuggled up to each other, like we had done for years when she was younger. As we talked, we both realized that it had been a very long time because the man who had been living with us had managed to put a wedge between us. In hindsight, we could see how he created situations with the purpose of eventually causing us to drift apart.

After a lot of cuddling, I got up to take care of a few things while Emily turned on the television and began flipping channels. I turned back toward the television and gasped, frozen in shock, as I saw a newsflash of the story to be aired later that night. There he was on the television screen, right before us, for all the world to see. He was in a courtroom, dressed in an orange jumpsuit, his hands and ankles restrained in handcuffs and shackles.

I hadn't seen Lawrence since he said good-bye as he pulled away with our boat on Sunday afternoon, and now here he was, in our family room. I heard the newscaster announce the upcoming story about him, but all I could see were big blotches of white. The next thing I knew, my mother, Emily, and Christopher were all squatted around me, telling me to wake up and asking me if I was okay. I could sense panic in their voices as they explained to me that I had passed out and hit the floor.

As strong as I wanted to be for my children, I was weak, I was exhausted, and I was overwhelmed and confused. My mother helped me into the bedroom, where she suggested I lie down and rest for a while as she cooked dinner. There I was once again, lying on my back and looking up toward the ceiling, helplessly, hopelessly in despair.

Not more than five minutes had gone by when the telephone rang. I rolled over and picked up the receiver. "Hello," I answered. The voice on the other end was not familiar, but the man referred to himself as a reporter from the newspaper. He was calling to get a statement from the family, he said.

I sobbed as I answered him. "How much more pain do you think we can handle? Any publicity would only cause more pain to the victim and the family!" And with that, I hung up the telephone. My body was shaking, and my voice was quivering as tears streamed down my face all over again.

As I lay there wondering how I could muster the strength to get up so I could tell my mother about the call and warn everyone not to answer the phone, the doorbell rang, and I also heard a knock on the front door. An adrenaline rush hit me like never before as I leapt off the bed and raced down the hallway to the front door. I stopped my mother just in the nick of time as I grabbed her arm and yelled, "Don't answer it! Don't answer it!"

I raced to the peephole in the door and looked out. As I'd suspected, it was the media. A female newscaster and her camera crew were standing at our front door. The microphone was at her mouth and the red light of the camera was running. They were waiting for me to open the door; they were waiting to expose our catastrophe to the rest of the world.

"They will have to get their ratings somewhere else," I said, "and not at our expense." And then I had a sudden thought. "Oh no, Mother! If they ruin the sale of this house, what will we do?"

My mother said, "I will handle this one." She opened the front door ever so slightly. "This house is for sale," my mother said to the newscaster, "and if you ruin the sale, we will sue you." Then she closed the door quickly, and we raced around the house, closing the curtains and blinds on every window. Suddenly, it dawned on me: we were the victims, yet we were also the ones in prison, right in our own home.

From one of the front bedroom curtains, I peeked out to see if the media had gone, only to find them standing in front of our neighbors' houses, interviewing every neighbor who was willing to walk outside and talk. Total exposure, shame, embarrassment, anger, fear, defenselessness, and a sense of hopelessness flooded my entire body. The world went about as if our pain was just another story. They failed to understand that, like a huge boulder thrown into calm water, the destructive quake of this man's actions had sent a brutalizing tsunami which ripped over and throughout every person's life that he had ever known.

Not more than ten or fifteen minutes later, the telephone began ringing again. "We will screen all our calls," I told my mother and the children. We gathered around the answering machine as it began to record. It was the realtor's voice, so my mother reached down and picked up the receiver.

The news was difficult to take. The realtor had received calls from the media, and they had informed him of the situation. My mother handed me the telephone, and the realtor said, "Wendy, I've been trying to reach you most of the day. I am so sorry to hear about what you are going through, but I cannot open escrow without a quitclaim deed signed by Lawrence."

I dropped my head in sorrowful despair, handing the phone back to my mother as I repeated what the realtor had said.

"Tomorrow is the Fourth of July. How are we going to do it?" my mother asked the realtor.

"I have a notary who is willing to help. She will meet us at the jail, if you think we can get it signed."

"Let's give it a try," my mother said, and they worked out the details of the when, where, and how.

I was blessed to have my mother staying with us, as the endless obstacles seemed much more than I could handle on my own. It was as if everywhere I turned, another problem fell down on top of me. *I need your help!* I cried out to God as I turned my face toward heaven. I knew it would take a miracle to get through this next dreadful thing I had to face: confronting the man who had destroyed our lives.

My alarm sounded early on Thursday morning, July 4. *Oh no,* I thought immediately, *I am not ready to face this day.* I was to meet the notary and the realtor at the jail. My body shook as I climbed out of bed; my anxiety was getting the best of me. *I must pull myself together,* I thought. *I have to get through this!*

It was clear the children and I had to move. The media had smeared our story all across the news. We were good, honest people, yet in the eyes of the world, we were tied directly to a man who committed unspeakably evil acts, which had damaged our family and shown him to be a threat to society. Being linked to him was taking us down as well, and we desperately needed to be set free.

Later that morning, I met the realtor and the notary, who were waiting for me outside the courthouse. I had called the jail ahead of time to ensure we'd be allowed to enter. My knees shook as I climbed the steps and we went inside to sit down. I noticed the realtor was sweating and had red blotches on his skin. It was apparent that the stress of the situation and the media involvement, along with the realization he was now doing business with a criminal and could possibly lose his sale, was causing his body to react. As he spoke nervously to me, I thought, *God, please help this man too.*

The jail personnel called my name when it was finally time for me to go in. I walked down the hall and through the door of a small room, about the size of a telephone booth, and my knees shook so fiercely that I thought they were going to shake right off. From around the corner, on the other side of the glass, I saw someone dressed in an orange jumpsuit, his face stricken with fear. It was the same jumpsuit I'd seen on the TV the night before when I fainted to the floor. It was the same man, Lawrence, although I felt I didn't know him anymore.

Awkwardly, I sat down on the stool at the counter. Then I nervously picked up the telephone receiver from the wall to talk with him. Tears ran down his checks as he looked into my eyes and told me how sorry he was. My pain and emotions surfaced as he spoke, and my own tears began to fall.

"How could you do it?" I whispered.

"I'm sorry. I'm sorry," he repeated.

I was so uncomfortable as I sat there across the glass from the man who had shattered our lives. My heart ached terribly, but I knew I had to gather myself together. I was sure that the realtor and notary were just as uncomfortable as I was and were anxiously waiting to take care of business so they could exit the premises as quickly as possible.

I explained that our realtor and his notary were with me because we had an offer on the house, but that the realtor would not open escrow without his signing a quitclaim deed.

"I've already discussed this with my attorney," Lawrence replied, "and my attorney has advised me not to sign."

Fear gripped my chest at his response. The thought of our being trapped in the house and community was more than I could fathom. I became lightheaded, and the hand that was holding the receiver went limp. The telephone dropped and clanged against the counter. I began to sob uncontrollably as I stood up, only to find myself too weak and overcome to remain standing. My knees buckled, and I dropped to the floor. On my knees, with tears running down my face, I raised my hands toward the glass dividing us, pleading with him to let us go.

"You said you were sorry! Please let us out! Please let us go!" I begged. "The media are circling us like sharks. They are standing at our front door with cameras. They are interviewing our neighbors. They are calling on the telephone. It's all over the newspaper headlines; it's on the five o'clock, six o'clock, ten o'clock, and eleven o'clock news! Please! Please let us free! It is as if we are in prison too. We are good people. We don't deserve this. Please let us go! We have hurt long enough! We are so ashamed and embarrassed; we can't even show our faces in town. We are being treated like we are freaks. Please, please sign the deed and let us free!"

I was crying so hard I could barely see his face through the glass. His head dropped forward as tears poured down his cheeks. It was as if the realization of what he had done and the devastating effects of it were beginning to take hold. "I will sign the deed," he said, as he waved to the officer behind the glass who was standing next to him. The officer escorted the notary behind the door and brought her over to him for the signature.

It was a miracle. Lawrence was signing the deed, and the children and I would be set free.

"I still need to talk to you," he said loudly to me as he finalized things with the notary.

I slowly pulled myself up off the floor and sat on the stool. I reached once again for the telephone receiver, planting my elbow on the counter so my arm wouldn't shake as I held the receiver up to my ear and waited.

As the notary left his area, Lawrence turned to face me and looked into my eyes, saying once again that he was sorry.

"You always promised me that you were faithful to me," I cried.

"But I was faithful to you!" he replied. With the most sincere look on his face, he added, "Nobody will ever love you as much as I do!"

I could not believe what I was hearing. A chill ran up and down my spine. *No, this cannot be happening,* I thought. *Does he really think that way? He abused my innocent child for years! Does he really believe he was faithful to me during all of that?* He could sense the shock on my face as I twitched in reaction to his comment.

"It's not my fault," he insisted. "She made me do it."

"What?"

"It was her fault," he said. "It was the way she looked at me."

My head was spinning out of control. Once again, I could not believe what I was hearing. Did he truly believe what he was saying? Was he actually blaming his destructive actions on the innocent eyes of a little child? How could I have ever thought I knew this man? I'd been so wrong; I never really knew him at all.

I was astonished at how he'd been able to hide such criminal and evil activity from me for all of the years of our marriage. On the other hand, I was amazed that he had signed the quitclaim deed, which truly was a miracle from God.

I thought of when the realtor told me we had an offer on the house, and I'd been confused about whether to stay or to sell. I had cried out to God for help and felt his answer—that it was time to sell the house. God must have known just how horrific things would become for my children and me. So much had happened in those two days since the realtor's call. God had told me over and over again that it was Independence Day. Now, it was the Fourth of July, and I realized that not only was God talking to me, but he also was telling me the truth—it actually was the Fourth of July, and it really was our own Independence Day.

Chapter 7

Breaking Free

It was now Friday morning, and the media was not about to let up, as we realized after seeing another front-page newspaper headline about the incident. It was as if they had taken a day off to celebrate the Fourth of July and then were back on track with the story. It was quickly apparent that today would be another day when we would remain inside the house with the curtains and blinds closed.

During breakfast, we received a call from Sandy, one of our many boating friends, who called to see if she could stop by for a few minutes. It was nice to hear from a friend, especially after feeling like prisoners in our own home, so we told her to please come right over.

We sat down at the kitchen table with Sandy, and she told us that our friends and their families had gathered together for the Fourth of July celebration. We were the topic of discussion, she said, and the group had elected Sandy to be their spokesperson to come over and find out how we were doing. They were mortified by the news and wanted to better understand what had happened as well. These friends consisted of six different families. My children and I met all of them when I married their best friend. Sandy explained how shocked and outraged they were—full of anger at a man they had known for years and entrusted with not only their own lives but also those of their children.

Sandy said that our friends were horror-struck by what my daughter had been through. They all adored her and were brokenhearted to find out about the years of manipulation, control, and destructive behavior to which she had been subjected. Tears of compassion welled in Sandy's eyes as she expressed their sorrow and regret, as well as her and our friends' outrage. Every positive thought of him had been washed away, leaving nothing but betrayal in its wake.

Our friends were troubled and confused by how well Lawrence had hidden the lies and secrets for so long. And unfortunately, a wave of insecurity crashed upon each family's heart as they questioned their own ability to truly know their own friends. They all found themselves wondering if they really knew the truth about each other's true identity. My heart went out to them too; our friends were experiencing pain as well.

After a couple hours of lengthy discussion, Sandy hugged each of us good-bye and once again expressed her and our other friends' sorrow and condolences. Then, Sandy looked directly into my eyes and confessed that she also had been assigned to find out if I had known all along of the abuse, because if I had known, they would have separated themselves from us immediately. But Sandy said she was convinced I had been fooled by this man's manipulative maneuvers as much as they were, and our friends were ready and willing to help us out in any way possible—all we had to do was ask.

I was terrified and relieved at the same time. I was thankful to God for friends who would come to see us and was even more thankful to God for friends who would now stand beside us. Family and friends continued to show up. They were compassionate and helped us out in our time of need. Once again, I could see the hand of God busily orchestrating his help from above.

During Sandy's visit, our telephone rang a couple of times, and people left voice messages, asking to view our home that was for sale. *How odd*, I thought. *How did they get our number, and why aren't they contacting our realtor instead?* After Sandy left, another call came in, and I recognized our realtor's voice leaving a message. I answered quickly, and the realtor then explained that our escrow had been opened. I was happy to hear it but then mentioned the earlier phone messages I'd received regarding viewing our home. The realtor assured me he would never give our personal phone number to anyone.

The telephone calls continued throughout the day. First, we had to stay inside and keep our curtains and blinds closed, but now these calls were tormenting us from the inside. My mother could see the frustration building within me after each new call. Finally, in desperation, I answered the telephone when it rang and asked the callers who they were, why they were calling, how they got my number. It didn't take long before I had it figured out—the callers were from the media; they wanted a way to get in the house; they wanted to get our story.

The badgering hit us from every side, and I was breaking down all over again. The children were worried and needed to feel safe, but it was hard to protect them when I was feeling so broken and defenseless myself. My mother could see my anxiety escalate, and panic was showing on her face as well.

"That's it!" my mother yelled. "We are out of here! Pack your bags quickly. I am taking you to my house!" My mother gave us specific instructions. "We need to move quickly. Put your bags by the door. I am going to back up my car in the driveway. As soon as I do, grab your bags, run, and jump in."

The house was already locked up tightly, and the front exit was ready. The children and I waited inside the front door, checking through the peephole while my mother turned the car around.

"It's time!" I yelled to the kids, and we ran out the front door and toward the car. "Watch your step!" We took off down the entry steps with our bags over our shoulders. We dove into my mother's car, hoping our neighbors wouldn't notice. "We made it!" I yelled, as my mother took off down the road. We'd done it; we'd broken free.

The following week was a blur of sleepless nights and many phone calls. Then, after returning home a little over a week later, we were greeted by family and friends from far and near. I was amazed at how many showed up to help us. I had no idea where the children and I would end up, so we each packed a suitcase and placed it in my mother's car for safekeeping. I wandered the house in shock and helpless confusion as everything was packed up and hauled to a storage unit within a few hours by our family and friends—that is, everything except for the family room furniture, as well as some other things that reminded us of "him"; those items were all left behind.

Upon returning home from my mother's house, we found our boat and truck had been completely stripped down inside and out and then driven back to the house and abandoned in front of my home by the in-laws. I was frightened and distressed as I faced the financial realization that everything falling onto my shoulders was a liability and much more than I could ever handle on my own. There were no assets associated to the lifestyle we had been living, as the loans were more than the sale values of our boat and vehicles. Amazingly, the kindness and help of our boating friends relieved the brunt of this painful realization.

A local boat dealer agreed to take the boat and sell it on their lot for me. They were terribly sorry about our tragedy and refused to take a dime for the ten months that it sat on their lot while waiting for a buyer. Eventually, they were able to sell it for a few thousand less than the loan I had on it, and they still refused to take a commission once it sold.

Alfred, a family friend, took our newly leased truck and sold it for me. I was afraid it would be terribly upside down, but he was able to get just eighteen dollars less than the financial obligation on it, which was such a blessing to me as well. Not only that, but he returned the check I gave him to cover all his other costs and advertising, saying I should spend it on my children.

Then there was Hank and Sandy, who were kind enough to use their trailer to pack our things and take the children, my mother, and me into their home for the remainder of our stay in town. They even insisted that we stay with them whenever we needed to return for the many hearings which lay ahead of us. God was definitely providing us with help and a way to break free from the numerous financial burdens.

With just a few days left before escrow would close, it was time to inform my employer that I would be moving out of town and not returning to work. It was a sad moment when I told the staff and hugged them good-bye, but they completely understood. They knew my family lived far way, and it would be best for us to relocate closer to them to have their support nearby.

Two days before escrow was to close, Emily and I met with one of the arresting officers at our house. We wanted to better understand what we should expect in the near future regarding the trials, and we were concerned for our safety, should either one of the men get out on bail. The officer was very helpful and answered all of our questions. He also felt that our moving away to be closer to a supportive family was a very good idea.

I will never forget one of the last things the officer told us. Surprisingly, he said only 5 percent of parents respond as I did upon learning their children have been abused. It is unfortunate, he explained, but sometimes the parent knows what is going on and refuses to acknowledge it, out of fear and possible loss—like the loss of a place to live or the loss of a partner. The truth is, they are afraid and do not know where they would go or what they would do if the facts were known, so they ignore it, pretending it's not happening, which only allows the abuse to continue.

The officer also said some parents never know of the abuse, but when they find out, they immediately accuse their children of lying. They cannot fathom that it might be true, or they fear the effect it will have on their own lives, or they just can't imagine the one being accused is actually capable of doing such a thing. But this is a subject rarely lied about, the officer explained, especially by children who wouldn't have the faintest idea what they are describing unless forced into such things. It gets very complicated, and perhaps that's the very reason why less than half the cases are ever reported.

Thriving on power and control, predators victimize not just the child but also anyone close who may thwart their tactics of fear, shame, and manipulation. There are rare but unfortunate occasions when the spouse's own insecurities actually cause him or her to blame the child instead of the abuser for what is happening.

"No!" I exclaimed. "A child is never responsible for a grown adult's actions!"

The officer's comments caused my mind to flash back to my own childhood for a brief moment. I was twelve years old, and it was my second day at a new school. During recess, I noticed a boy I thought was very handsome, and I smiled at him. Shortly afterward, he and a dozen other boys walked up and cornered me against the building. The boy I had smiled at proceeded to put his hands up my blouse and all over while the others surrounded us, ensuring no one else on the playground could see. Thank goodness the recess bell rang; it was the only thing that stopped the torment.

That event was in no way comparable to what Emily had gone through, yet the shameful disgrace and effect it had on me was astounding. I never told anyone what happened for over twelve years. Only after I had a child was I able to admit it, which is exactly how long it took to finally realize it was not my fault. At the time, I was too ashamed to tell anyone. Somehow, I thought it must have been my fault, because I smiled at him in the first place and invited the abuse. I ended up refusing to go back to school and constantly cried that the homework was too difficult. I was eventually taken to a psychiatrist, whose office window happened to overlook the schoolyard where the abuse had taken place. This only caused me to freeze up even more. After a nightmare of attempts by my parents to get me back to school, I ended up with a tutor for the rest of the year and then transferred to a private school in town the following year. My parents perceived me as a difficult yet fragile child, but abuse was never questioned or queried. I suggested to the officer that perhaps a large number of the abused do not speak up because they somehow feel it must have been their own fault and are plagued with undeserved humiliation, fear, shame, or guilt. There seems to be one common thread—an uninvited touch and the choice of another to act.

Immediately, a burning desire flooded my body. I wanted to make every person in the world aware that an abuser or predator must be held accountable for his or her own actions and stopped at any cost. *Yes, that is exactly what needs to take place in this world,* I thought. *And more important, the abused must be set free.*

I am eternally grateful that my daughter had the courage to speak up and tell the truth. I am so thankful she is no longer being abused, and I am no longer attached to a man of deceit, living in the midst of deception. The only way to stop tragedies such as this is by speaking up and telling the truth. Then others must believe, accept, and correct the injustice. We must stop the lies, destructive secrets, and abuse.

I am reminded of a saying I once heard: "The truth will set you free" (John 8:32 NIV). Those words could not be more true. Oh, how I hope every victim will have the courage, like my daughter, to boldly speak up and tell the truth, and oh, how I hope every parent or person told has the strength and valor to receive it and the ability and power to put a stop to it.

Unfortunately, as I came to understand, in the United States alone, one in three women will be sexually abused during their lifetimes. And one in four women and one in six men will be sexually assaulted before the age of eighteen. Did you know that every two minutes someone, somewhere in America is sexually violated? And approximately two-thirds of the assaults are committed by someone known to the victim?[1] It is such a horrendous crime yet kept so shamefully

---

[1]   WOAR (Women Organized Against Rape) September 2015 - woar.org/resources/sexual-assault-statistics.php

secret. More victims keep quiet about the abuse received than those who tell. No wonder it runs rampant and so many get away with it. It is estimated that 68 percent of all assaults will never be reported to the police, and 98 percent of all rapists will never spend a day in jail for their crime.[2] Something more needs to be done, my heart cried out. Something more needs to be done.

We thanked the officer for his time, and he wished us both well. Once again he expressed appreciation to Emily for her bravery and strength in speaking up and telling the truth.

I picked up my purse and put my arm around Emily as we headed toward the front door. We were leaving the empty house for the very last time. I turned and looked back across the rooms one more time. Quietly, I said to myself, "Good-bye house, good-bye secrets, and good-bye abuse. You can't have your way with us any longer."

The day finally arrived when the buyers would be depositing their funds into escrow, and the sale of the house would be closed. Once that was done, the children and I would head south to stay with my mother for a while. My mother had already left town ahead of us to prepare for our arrival. We had decided to stay with her until we could determine where we should live, as well as allowing ourselves time to heal.

I had family members to the north and south, and each suggested we move to their town. But the reality was, we were very broken, and I was in no shape to look for a job or a place to live at the moment. The shock and sudden loss made it difficult to think clearly. I had completely lost my appetite and was weak and overwhelmed. The thought of being strong

---

[2]   RAINN (Rape, Abuse & Incest National Network) September 2015 - rainn.org/statistics

and interviewing for a job or looking for a new place to live was more than I could imagine. All I knew was we needed to leave this place and start over, and I couldn't do it on my own. I most definitely needed help.

On the day when we should have been closing on the house, my realtor called me at Sandy's, his voice full of panic.

"It's the buyers," he said. "They have refused to place their funds into escrow! They found out whose house they are buying. They know all about Lawrence and his crime, and they said they won't deposit any funds into escrow unless you accept their reduced sale price."

The buyers' insistence on reducing the purchase price to an astronomically low amount meant there would not be much left to take with us after paying off the current loan on the house. I was frightened because I knew I would need money to care for the children and help us survive while I pulled myself back together and rebuilt our lives.

Now, I found myself filled with anger. "That's not fair!" I cried to the realtor. "How can they do that? They are taking advantage of our catastrophe. They expect to pay tens of thousands less than market value, all because they know I need to sell, and they know how desperate I am." I yelled, I screamed, I cried. Feelings of despair overwhelmed me as I thought how trapped I felt and how badly we needed to be gone. How would I survive and take care of the children and myself? We had nothing but our suitcases and a few household items in a storage unit. "Oh, how will we survive?" I cried over and over again.

I was so distraught after ending the call with my realtor that I immediately called my father. I wept profusely. "What do I do? It's not fair! How can they be so cruel? They agreed to more, and I agreed to cover a new roof and all the other little things they asked for. What do I do, Dad?" As we talked, I realized I had to sell.

It was more important that I accept the price and leave town quickly, ensuring the children's and my safety. The reality was I could not financially handle the expenses of the home on my own. Even if I could, we were trapped inside the house and could not open our curtains without the media and others looking and casting judgment. The thought of my children trying to face other children when school started was another window of fear I could not even begin to open. The last thing I wanted was for them to be embarrassed or humiliated. We had to go, and that meant I had to accept the buyers' ridiculously low and unjust price. We would have a little left over after the sale or at least enough to cover some legal fees and bare essentials for a couple of months. Discouraged yet resolved, I called the realtor back and gave him the okay.

As I drove toward the escrow company where I would sign the final papers, I cried to God once again. "God, I believe you heard my cry earlier, and I can undeniably see that you have been answering me ever since. But God, I am scared right now, and I don't understand what is happening, nor do I know how the children and I are going to survive. You have proven you are big enough to stop the pain, abuse, secrets, and lies when I asked for your help, so perhaps I need to start trusting in you every day and believing that somehow you will continue to help us. The truth, God, is that I need you. I cannot do this on my own. Please keep listening, and please keep answering. Please don't ever leave me, because I don't want to do it without you. And God ... I really do want you to know I am so very sorry that I didn't choose you sooner."

Chapter 8

Heading South

It was late at night when we finally arrived at my mother's house, suitcases in hand, fragile and distraught. It was also the second time we had ever been to her home, although the first was a blur. It was a beautiful two-story home with lots of windows, white carpet, and dark wood floors. It was a relief to finally see her smiling face when we arrived. We were terribly exhausted and immediately headed up stairs toward the guest room/office with our things. Once we set our things down, my mother made us each a cup of hot herbal tea. It was so comforting to wrap my fingers around the cup as we sat at her kitchen table, discussing the overwhelming events which had transpired throughout the day.

The children and I had each brought one suitcase of clothes, along with some toiletry items. I had hoped it would be enough to get us by until such time as we could make arrangements for a more permanent place to live. My mother gave us blankets to make beds on the floor, and my daughter insisted on sleeping next to me. I loved that she wanted to stay close to me, yet I ached for the reasons she so desperately required that closeness.

On the third morning after our arrival, I found myself tossing and turning, unable to sleep any longer. My heart ached terribly, and between the feeling in the pit of my stomach and the heaviness in my chest, I was reminded of my devastating level of sorrow, pain, and loss. A shocking sensation of disbelief kept running through my head, and continual attacks of fear swept through my mind. I couldn't seem to stop the endless thoughts of what Emily had been through. I kept asking myself, *Why did this have to happen? What is going to come next?*

Because I was unable to sleep, I decided to get up shortly after six o'clock and go to the kitchen. I thought a hot cup of tea sounded comforting, and maybe its warmth would help settle my aching heart.

I quietly slipped out of the room, hoping not to wake the children. I could tell my mother was sound asleep too, for total silence greeted me as I entered the hallway and quietly tiptoed toward the staircase. I took a few steps, but then found myself stopping to look up. There were rays of sunlight shining through the skylight in the hallway above the landing. They were bouncing against the high walls, causing the white carpet to glisten. Looking up, it dawned on me: we were homeless!

With all the commotion of trying to leave, it hadn't hit me the way it did now. Once again, panic gripped me tightly, and I froze right where I was standing on the stairs. I grabbed the railing to keep myself from falling as I bent over and quietly cried out in pain. "The kids and I are homeless! We are homeless!" My knees began to buckle, and I sank down on the stairs. With my head leaning against the railing and my hands gripping it for dear life, I lay on the stairs weeping uncontrollably and muttering repeatedly, "We are homeless. We are homeless. I've never been homeless before in my life. I have two children to care for, and we are homeless."

I don't know how long I sat there crying, but eventually I continued down the stairs, with eyes blurred from tears and overwhelming anguish. As I walked toward the kitchen, I felt an urge to glance across the family room. My eyes were drawn to the large wall-to-wall bookcases that stood from floor to ceiling on each side of the fireplace. Without reason, I found myself scanning the bookshelves until my eyes fell upon a huge white book in the far left corner—the largest in the bookcase. It was our old family Bible, something I hadn't seen in over twenty years.

I was compelled to pull it from the shelf, and it took all my strength to carry the large Bible to the coffee table, where I set it down. Still weepy and feeling weak, I exhaustedly flopped onto the couch, reached out, and randomly opened the Bible. As I looked down at its pages, everything was blurred through my tears—but red letters popped off the page which read "Let not your heart be troubled ..."

These words brought even more uncontrollable sobbing, for my heart was extremely troubled. How did this book know? I shook my head slightly, hoping somehow it would clear my vision, but it didn't. I looked down again, and more red-letter words popped out.

"I go to prepare a place for you." The message shocked me, and through my clouded vision I tried to focus once again, only to see the new words that read "If it were not so, I would have told you" (John 14:1–2 KJV).

"God, is that you?" I whispered. "God, are you talking to *me*?" As soon as I asked, an instantaneous warmth ran through my being, from head to toe, like warm, thick honey running through the inside and consuming me—like I had experienced in the shower earlier when I heard the words "Independence Day." I knew it was God talking to me. There was absolutely no doubt. *God is here*, I realized. *God is with me! He knows I am crying! He knows my pain!*

"God, you heard my cry once again, and you are answering me, aren't you? I think you're telling me you are taking care of things, and we will be all right. Your words are so comforting and so reassuring, more than a cup of tea could ever be. You really do care about us, don't you, God?" Tears poured down my face as an unexplainable joy filled my heart, and an amazing peace came over me.

I had done nothing to deserve this, yet God cared about me—about us, about our pain, about our loss. Not only did God hear the cries of my heart that no other could understand, but God answered me, comforted me, and reassured me. I experienced God's loving me. A soft, sweet smile came over my face, and an unbelievable weight lifted from my shoulders. I leaned back on the couch, and a huge sigh of relief slowly released from within.

I had never experienced God like this before. I grew up in a family that belonged to a very regimented and formal religion. God was more of a mystery to me, and my knowledge of him led me to believe he was more of an almighty authoritarian, an all-powerful one, who was quick to lay judgment and whose job was to inflict punishment. Later, in my teens, my family transitioned to a different denomination. In both cases, I seemed to have an intellectual knowledge of God, but now, this was completely different. This was personal. This was intimate, and unlike anything I had ever experienced.

I felt loved and cared for, as if I was someone God already knew intimately and for whom he had a genuine affection and concern. Not only had God heard and answered my first cry for help, miraculously ending our nightmare, but now God was telling me he would help the children and me put our lives back together. I began to see a God who was compassionate and complete, one whose intention was to finish what he had begun.

It is difficult to put into words the peace which came over me and the instantaneous outpouring of love and compassion that flooded my heart and soul. I had an overwhelming desire to know God, and after experiencing his loving me so deeply, I wanted nothing more than to love him right back. This amazing love I received slowly created a newfound confidence in me, as if I truly mattered, like a peasant girl who discovers she actually is the daughter of a king.

As soon as the children and my mother awoke, I was excited to share the event I had just experienced. I assured the children we would be all right and told them, "I don't know where we will live, and I don't know when I will be ready to find us a home, but I am confident in this: when it is time and wherever we end up looking, there will be a home waiting for us."

I knew I had heard from God, and it gave me comfort, but as days progressed into weeks, I found myself buried in a slew of financial issues that became nightmares. There were accounts that needed to be changed or closed, bills to be paid, address changes, and health insurance coverage transfers that had to be made, ensuring my children remained covered. It was a lot for someone with a clear head, and I was far from that.

My shock was evident with every phone call I made. There wasn't one person on the other end of the telephone who didn't hear my helpless regurgitating of the events leading to my need to call. It was like listening to the same hysterical recording over and over, yet I couldn't seem to stop. I found myself breaking down in tears every time I made a new call.

The simplest of roadblocks, ones under normal circumstances I would have solved quickly, threw me spinning and spiraling downward into an emotional crash. Each little thing to be handled seemed much more than I could possibly manage. There were days when I would sit in the middle of my mother's living room with papers and files spread across the carpet, and all I could do was cry. I felt hopelessly overwhelmed and completely out of control. The way I was handling things was so opposite from the person I used to be. It was quickly apparent the adrenaline I had been running on had completely run out.

The Victim Witness Program allotted funds to cover counseling visits for people in our situation, and the three of us were quickly set up for individual appointments. Due to the critical state we were in, we were scheduled for counseling three times a week. The emotional breakdowns were constant, and the realities of life were catching up with us.

We got sick often, and within the first four weeks I had lost twenty pounds. I couldn't sleep, and I couldn't eat. I was heartbroken and going through a large array of emotions. Feeling sick to my stomach and mentally exhausted became the norm. Watching the pain and agony my children were going through was the worst part of it.

Through counseling I learned to write down my feelings, a healing technique I used often in the beginning, as it helped me sort through the confusion. A month into our tragedy I wrote this:

> *Someday I will wake up in the morning and not think about what you were doing to my daughter.*
> *Someday I will wake up in the morning, and my heart will not be filled with sorrow, loss, and grief.*
> *Someday I will wake up in the morning and not wonder how I am going to get through the day or*

wonder where I am going to live or work or where I should put the children in school.

Someday I will not wake up with my chest aching, wondering if you really ever loved me, not understanding how I could have loved you so much and trusted you with all my heart and now be so afraid to ever trust again.

Someday I will go to bed at night, not afraid of a new day to come.

Someday I will go to bed at night and not look at my daughter and wonder just how much pain she is really in or fear for her future.

Someday, I will go to bed at night without all the tears, the sorrow, and pain.

Each day I pray God will heal all our hearts. That he will ease the pain. That he will guide and direct our lives ... the rest of our days.

In spite of my assurance from God that the children and I would eventually have a home again, the days at my mother's place turned into weeks and then months. The pain and agony never seemed to let up. I realized the healing process was filled with continuous baby steps, and it was going to take a lot longer than I had ever expected.

One thing was certain: I could not have made it without help. My parents and my family, as well as dear friends and acquaintances along the way, continually supported and encouraged us to keep going.

If it were not for the word of promise I felt I had received from God that we would have a place to live again someday, I most likely would have given up the fight and completely given up on the idea of ever pulling through this ordeal.

Chapter 9

A Cup of Coffee

One of the first outings my mother took the children and me on was to a small coastal village near her house known for its boutiques, art galleries, and seafood restaurants. She was attempting to change our thoughts from the constant sense of pain and loss, if only for a moment. She took us to a beautiful restaurant that served Greek food on the edge of the water, but I couldn't eat. When my mother tried to get me to at least nibble on the food, I wasn't even able to chew. As the children ate their meals, their eyes looked toward me in despair. I could tell it was difficult—even frightening—for them to see me this way, which broke my heart even more.

After dinner, my mother led us through the tiny gift and art shops in the village. They were lit up beautifully, but I could think only that the things we saw in the shops didn't really matter. How could stuff matter at a time like this? *Besides, I thought, what good are any of these things if we don't have a home to put them in? What's more, I don't have a job, so I couldn't buy it if I liked it anyway.*

A very distinct change took place within me on July 1, and ever since, my priorities became completely different. All at once, the little things that used to matter so much meant nothing compared to the safety of my children, our lives, and how we would survive. My attitude switched from always trying to please others or focusing on material things to only wanting the children and me to be safe.

As we continued through the shops, I could barely walk. I was lifeless, using what little strength remained to lift my head occasionally, mustering a smile to my mother or children in the hope of relieving their concerns.

The night air was cool and moist, and as we walked up to a little outdoor café, my mother exclaimed, "Would anyone like a hot decaf? Or how about a hot mocha? It's my treat!" I knew she was attempting to delight us.

Looking up, I watched as a customer accepted a hot mocha; it was covered in whipped cream and was piping hot—steam rose from the cup. I thought, *I'm so cold, and that big coffee cup looks so warm and inviting.* "Thanks, Mom," I responded. "I think I would like a hot mocha."

Smiling at me, she ordered a hot decaf mocha with lots of whipped cream.

With the first sip, I closed my eyes. Its warmth brought to mind the comfort I'd known when I had felt God speak to me—first in the shower, confirming that we needed to sell the house and claim our independence, and then through his words in our family Bible, promising me he had a place for us. The warmth of the coffee was a reminder of God's promises to me.

My thoughts were interrupted by my mother's question. "How is your mocha?"

I looked up at her with a smile. "It's wonderful; thank you so much." Yes, it truly was wonderful. Our world had been swept away, but somehow, I was finding comfort in the way God was helping me and touching my heart, as well as through this hot cup of coffee that felt so comforting in my hands.

A few days later, after a counseling session, my mother took us on another adventure to the zoo. She was desperately trying to get our minds on to new things, like God's beauty and the wonders of nature.

It was a beautiful summer day and a weekday, so the crowds were light. The sights were enjoyable, but every breath I took caused a pain that ached all the way to my soul. My inability to eat and sleep, along with losing twenty pounds—and I already had been thin—left my body frail and weak. Life had become a moment-by-moment struggle for survival.

The zoo was large and took an enormous effort to get from one attraction to another. When we arrived at a moving sidewalk that went for a large stretch up the hillside, I took advantage and sat down on the moving rubber runner for the long haul up the hill. It was a little embarrassing to be sitting, but I needed to take this moment of rest.

As I sat there, all I could think was that I had lost everything except my children, and even they had been taken from me for a moment. With no home and no job, I was frightened, alone, and didn't know where I belonged—or even if "belonging" was an option any more. How quickly I kept forgetting all that God had done so far.

On the moving sidewalk, I pulled a notepad from my purse and wrote a little message to myself of my heart's desire: *All I want in life is a cup of coffee, with a side of job and a little house for dessert.* I could not have been more real, more direct, or more helpless in that moment.

The truth was that within myself, I could not find the motivation to keep going. It was my children and their desperate need to survive and my love for them that kept me moving forward. *Perhaps*, I thought, *God desperately loves us too, and that is why he's been speaking to my heart and answering our cries for help.*

It wasn't long before we received notice from the district attorney that we were needed for a bail reduction hearing at the county courthouse where the arrest had taken place. "There is a chance the bail could be reduced from two million," the district attorney informed me on the telephone. "We need you and your daughter to attend this hearing."

The possibility of this man getting out on bail sent terror through me. Would he run if he made bail? If that happened, I feared he'd be angry, possibly spiteful, and maybe even attempt to come after us. I was trying not to show my fear as I informed the children and my mother, but inside, I felt paralyzed.

Our friends Hank and Sandy invited us to stay with them once again while we were in town, and the volunteer coordinator from my previous employment offered to drive us to the hearing. As I sat in the backseat on the way to the courthouse, I cried to God in my head. *Oh God, please don't let his bail be reduced. I am so afraid for our safety if he gets out!*

At that moment, I heard a distinct voice in my head respond. *"His bail will be reduced, but do not worry. I am in control."* The answer I received astonished me, yet gave me peace— and I held tightly onto that. *If this is true*, I thought, *then I am extremely grateful to know ahead of time that God is in control and will work it out. Otherwise, I would be terrified, overwhelmed, and completely fall apart.*

Emily and I sat in a tiny waiting room. Due to our fragile state, the judge and the attorneys decided to proceed with negotiations without our direct presence in the courtroom. I was grateful we were spared from having to look at this guilty man's face, as my heart could not take it, and Emily didn't deserve to go through that pain and punishment any longer.

After a lengthy deliberation, the district attorney informed us the bail had been cut in half to one million. Our immediate response was panic. Between his parents, siblings, daughter from a prior marriage, and whatever other funds he had available to him, the bail bond—the percentage of the amount required—could be reached. I took a deep breath, and a peace came over me as I remembered God's voice reassuring me, "His bail will be reduced, but do not worry. I am in control." I closed my eyes and held on to those words, repeating them in my mind.

The interesting thing is that even though he could have made the new bail bond amount, he did not. Ultimately, he did not receive assistance with his bail. The bail reduction may have been the best thing that happened to him because it forced him to deal with the choices he made, the truth of his guilt, and the consequences of his actions.

My mother greeted us with a hug when we returned to her house. It was nice to be back, even if that meant our days would be filled with continued counseling and doctor appointments. On the way home from one of those appointments, I asked my mother if she would take me to a Christian bookstore in the area. I didn't have much money, but knew I wanted a Bible. I wanted to learn more about this God who was speaking to my heart, who was bringing comfort and encouragement in the midst of my storms, and who was answering my prayers, one after another.

Glancing at the available Bibles on the shelf, I noticed a tiny—three inches by four and half inches—New Testament with Psalms. It didn't cost too much and was the perfect size to fit in my purse and always be with me. I eagerly purchased the little book, desperately wanting to know more about this loving God.

I had seen glimpses of hope as I saw God work in our lives, but my emotional status was still a pendulum, swinging back and forth with each new challenging circumstance. One evening, sitting in the backseat of my mother's car, my emotions once again got the best of me. It was late, and I was tired, but even more so, I was going through another wave of internal breakdown. I didn't want my children to see me this way, so I turned my head away to wipe the tears from my eyes. Would I recover enough to be the strong mother my children needed?

Thoughts of how every important man in my life ended up leaving had me questioning my significance and value. I was struggling with my identity, questioning who I was and if I really mattered or was capable of anything worthwhile. I felt alone and feared for our futures.

As tears ran down my face, I cried out inside, *God, who am I to you? Do I really even matter? What is going to happen to us? How do I know we will be safe? Will we be okay?* All of a sudden I felt a nudging to pull the little pocket Bible from my purse. Opening it, I saw these words: "To the elect [chosen] lady and her children, whom I love in truth, and not only I, but also all those who have known the truth, because of the truth which abides in us and will be with us forever: Grace, mercy, and peace will be with you from God the Father and from the Lord Jesus Christ, the Son of the Father, in truth and love" (2 John 1:1–3 NKJV).

A warm comfort came over me, and the heaviness instantly lifted. Surprise filled my heart as I focused on the words relating to a woman and her children. What were the chances of opening this little book and having it speak directly to me? Not only did the words identify us, a mother and her children, but they promised love, truth, mercy, and grace.

The word "truth" kept spinning in my head. The God who had been making his presence felt in my life had opened the doors of truth, exposing the lies and setting us free. These words also spoke of others who would know the truth and love us too. The words promised grace, mercy, and peace directly from God the Father and his Son Jesus Christ.

I thought of how many times I had looked to another individual in my life, wanting to believe that person could fulfill my deepest desire and need to feel chosen, adored, and wanted, only to be let down, time and again. I had spent my life pleasing and serving, hoping to be worthy of acceptance and approval, but each time I thought I had found what I was searching for, it seemed to leave as quickly as it came. Now, God was offering his love and acceptance for free, without my earning it or proving I was good enough to receive it.

These few words in my little Bible gave me exactly what I needed: hope. This message was tangible, something I could hold on to, just like the words God gave me about preparing a place for us to live. I was absolutely convinced the words were exactly what God wanted me to see and know. It was as if God the Father and his Son Jesus Christ were letting me know that no matter how many times I had been abused or abandoned, betrayed, or rejected, in God's eyes I was wanted and chosen. But this promise was not just for me; my children were included in these compassionate words of love and desire as well.

The love and acceptance I experienced with God ignited a deepening hunger and desperate desire to know and understand more about this God and his Son, who obviously already knew so much more about me. Yes, in a way, God was like a cup of coffee—I was getting a taste of something wonderful in the midst of nothing. He was bringing warmth, comfort, and a sense of belonging to my soul.

Chapter 10

A Side of Job

The new school year was about to begin, yet we were not at the point where we could be on our own. I was still experiencing an emotional roller coaster, and the children and I still attended counseling sessions three times a week. I constantly battled feelings of loss and confusion, and the thought of getting a job and a place to live was much too impossible to fathom.

My mother took us to school and assisted me with the children's enrollment. It was quite a distance from her house. There was graffiti covering the walls and fences around the school and schoolyard. We felt we were walking into a foreign culture. *This will be a temporary arrangement*, I thought. Within a few days after the school session began, we transferred the children to another school on the other side of the school district. The children and I sat down with the new school counselor, briefly explaining the trauma we had been through and asking her to work through the difficulties with us.

The second school felt safer than the first, but the children were having a terrible time adjusting. One of Christopher's first school assignments was to write about his strongest impression of his new school. His words expressed disappointment; he missed the community we'd come from, his friends, and where he had once felt accepted. As I read his writing, it broke my heart all over again. As I tucked Christopher into bed that night, I asked him to please tell me what was wrong. He answered, "Everything." He felt his life had been pulled out from under him; it had been ruined, and no matter what I did, where I got a new job, or wherever we decided to live, he felt it was too late. We'd gone through so much pain and loss together, but we also were affected individually. The three of us desperately needed to fit in again, and even more so, we each needed to feel safe, secure, accepted, and wanted.

Every new day at their second school brought another day of difficulty and grief. Instead of things getting easier, every day brought a deeper sense of not fitting in or belonging, even more than the day before. It tormented my heart to see them struggle so greatly. As days turned into weeks, my need to protect them became greater than my need to heal or hide from the world that had crushed us so deeply, so I called a family meeting. I asked Emily and Christopher, "Where do you want to live? Because wherever you pick, we will go there. I will find the strength within me. I will pull myself together, and I will ask God for his help. Whatever it takes to get my résumé together and look for a job, I will do it. I just need to know where I should start looking, so where should it be, kids?"

The children immediately chimed in unison, "We want to live near Uncle Brad and Aunt Amy!"

"Then it's settled," I said. My older brother, Brad, and his wonderful wife, Amy, lived in a beautiful area about an hour and a half north of my mother's place. I was so very happy when Amy became a part of our family, and the three of us had a close relationship when they were first married. We drifted apart, though, after my brother took a job in the southern part of the state and moved away, years earlier.

The children and I had enjoyed a few visits with them over the past couple of months. They were always caring and very supportive. Our visits never failed to include a mention of how much they would love to have us live near them. My brother and Amy's children were around the same age as my kids, so moving close to them meant my children also would have cousins nearby. My brother was great at getting all of us outside, doing something healthy and active, every time we got together. He was either taking us to the beach or getting us to join him in a game of Ultimate Frisbee. Amy, on the other hand, was a gentle pillar of strength. Her compassionate heart and prayerful words brought comfort each time we visited.

Our minds were made up, so I began working feverishly on my résumé—but I found myself struggling. I begged God for the strength and willpower to keep going. At first, I had to ask my family for their help in preparing the résumé, because I found it too overwhelming to do on my own. But almost continuously, I asked God for his help and direction. I was convinced that this God I was getting to know was truly for me and not against me. And the more I turned to him for help, the more empowered I was to keep going. I was convinced that I needed him more than anything else to survive. Somehow, I knew in my heart there was hope, if only I could hold on to this God of love and mercy, who had so graciously brought us this far.

The world was such a difficult place for me, yet the more I stayed focused on God and the love and desire I had to care for and protect my children, the more I had the strength to press onward. Although I felt broken and incapable, the love I had for my children gave me the much needed strength to work day after day until finally, my résumé was completely pulled together and ready to distribute. There was a joy that came from accomplishing this feat, and I was extremely grateful to all who had helped, especially God.

Getting my résumé together was only the first of many baby steps in making a change toward a new job, home, and life. Now I had to figure out the next step and how I would proceed. Just the thought of moving forward overwhelmed me. I learned to turn to others for encouragement, but the fear and anxiety were always present. I decided I needed to turn to the God who had listened and had answered thus far. I prayed intently that night before going to sleep and asked God to please help me find a job. I even tried to reason with God as I literally begged him, "God, you must have a job out there somewhere for me, or how else would we be able to have a home again—you know, the one you promised when you said you had a place prepared for us?" My cries to God continued with tears running down my checks. I prayed and asked for strength, courage, and the wisdom required to make it through this search.

The next morning I woke up with a very strong impression of how to begin. On Monday morning, I was to drive up to my brother and sister-in-law's house with a stack of my résumés. I was to pick up a map of their local area and go through the telephone book to find all the health care companies within the area. For each company for which I felt I might be qualified to work, I was to mark the location on the map. After that, I was to drive from place to place, introduce myself, and hand them a copy of my résumé. I was to explain to them that I was moving into the area and would like to know if they had any positions available for which my skills might be suited.

It was early Monday morning when I dropped the children off at school. I assured them I would be heading directly to their aunt and uncle's place to start looking for a job so we could relocate. I told the children, "I am not sure how late it will be before I get back, so your grandmother will pick you up at school today." They didn't say it, but the look in their eyes said it all—they were begging me to hurry and find a job and get them out of this school. The look brought anguish to my heart, yet at the same time, it empowered me like never before. I had to start putting our lives back together again.

I headed up the coast, talking to God all the way. "God, you have helped us thus far, and I know it must break your heart like it breaks mine to see my children in such pain and misery. Please help me to find the right job and in the right location. Please give me the strength and courage to do this. Please ..." An unexplainable comfort and peace came over me. Somehow, although I was alone, I did not feel alone, and I knew God was with me, listening to everything I had to say to him.

Brad and Amy greeted me with big smiles and warm hugs when I arrived. I felt so welcome and quickly went to work, matching up companies in the area to locations on the map and then identifying the route I would take to visit them all. Before driving off, Amy sat down with me and said a prayer. Then, I drove around to each company, one by one, handing out my résumé and introducing myself. At the end of the day, before heading back to my mother's, I sat down with Amy at her kitchen table to discuss the day's events. She prayed with me once again, thanking the Lord for his help and strength with my job search.

The next morning, I received a call from the owner of a company that was only three miles from my brother's house. As it turned out, she had a manager position available, so we set up an appointment for an interview the following day, Wednesday. Shortly after that phone call, I received another call from a second company, which had a position opening up in their regional office about twenty minutes north of my brother's place. I set up an appointment for an interview with them on Friday.

When I updated the children with the good news, smiles lit up their faces, and that gave me hope. Yet I had two deep-seated fears that haunted me. One of my largest challenges since July 1 had been my inability to remember things, and I wondered how I would be able to work at any job. The severe shock I went through had caused a wall to go up in my mind, blocking memories and all the events that led up to my pain. Unfortunately, it affected both my long- and short-term memory. Sometimes the children would complain that I didn't listen to them, but I just wasn't able to remember what they'd said. The post-traumatic effects were explained to me in counseling as my body's way of preserving itself. It was hoped that it would improve with time.

My second concern was the numbness in my pinky and ring fingers on my left hand. They became numb the day I went to the county jail and spoke on the wall-mounted handset. It must have been caused by the way I drilled my elbow down into the counter as I nervously spoke through the phone. It had been an enormously emotional day—that was when I'd begged him to sign the quitclaim deed. I worried and wondered how I could type or work efficiently on a computer with two fingers numb on my dominant side.

On Wednesday morning, I stopped by my brother's house on the way to my first interview, and Amy prayed with me. She had the spiritual faith I wanted for myself.

The interview went well, but I returned to my mother's place uncertain of its outcome. On Thursday morning, I received a call with an offer for the job. I accepted the position, grateful to have found a job so quickly and one that was located so close to Brad and Amy's home. The job would begin on November 1, giving us only a couple of weeks to find a new place to live in the area.

My mother and children were very excited when I told them the good news. "I better cancel the interview for Friday," I told them as I quickly dashed into the other room. I called the woman who had scheduled my Friday interview and apologized for the cancellation. I explained the new position I had just accepted. She understood and wished me well.

I went to bed that Thursday night in total amazement. As I thought back over the week, I realized how quickly things had evolved. I had searched for a job on Monday, and by Tuesday I had two interviews lined up. I interviewed on Wednesday and landed a job on Thursday. I was so excited to be able to miraculously step forward as I needed to do. As I closed my eyes, these thoughts kept spinning through my mind, but with each new breath, I was able to slowly unwind. I went to sleep, filled with gratitude and with a heart that thanked God for his awesome provision and astonishing help. I was beginning to understand that my God was not only my comforter but my provider as well.

Chapter 11

A Little House for Dessert

Now that I had a job lined up, the next thing on the immediate list was to find a home. I called Brad and Amy to tell them the good news and to thank Amy for her prayers. I also asked for their assistance in locating a rental home in their area.

Amy told me the real estate section of the paper with the new rentals came out every Saturday morning, so the children and I made plans to be there first thing Saturday morning and check the new listings.

I made a list of what we needed in a home, hoping and praying that the home would

1. be within walking distance to the children's school, as I would be at work until after five each weeknight;
2. be within walking or biking distance to Brad and Amy's house, so they could go there after school if they wanted to;
3. have a garage so I didn't have to pay for an additional storage unit, as I needed the time and space to go through our belongings before I would know what to do with them; and

4. be a place where we could have a dog, as my daughter
    had always wanted one.

Brad and Amy welcomed us with open arms, which
included lots of smiles, big hugs, and excited congratulations.
Amy had already looked through the paper and other local
publications. She found only one townhome listed for rent in
the area, but it had three bedrooms and a two-car garage and
was about two miles west of their home. The school that the
children would attend sat right in the middle, about a mile
from each.

The townhome sounded like it could work, but I was
worried about the rent and initial deposit. So I looked at
the price of two- and three-bedroom apartments without
a garage, as well as a couple single-family homes for rent in
the outlying areas, but they were even more costly. It became
apparent that although the townhome seemed high-priced
for me, it was probably the best-priced rental available in the
area.

I felt an urgency to go for it, so I quickly called the
telephone number listed in the advertisement. There was no
answer, so I left a voice message, saying I was very interested
in looking at the property. A couple hours went by, during
which we drove around the area while we waited to hear back.
Finally, I became nervous that it had already been rented, so
I called the number once again.

This time, a man answered the telephone. He explained
that he was the owner of the property and had received
my earlier message. He had not called me back because the
tenants who were currently occupying the townhome and
who had just given their thirty-day notice to leave were too
sick to let people see the place that day. I could see it, he said,

two days later, on Monday evening between six and six thirty. I told the owner I would be there.

As soon as the children got out of school on Monday, we drove back to Brad and Amy's home. Amy had invited us for dinner, which we enjoyed quickly, but we were eager to see this one and only place that was available in the immediate area—and the only one that came close to meeting our needs. Brad and Amy told us to jump in their van, and we all headed off to see the townhome.

When we arrived, much to my dismay, there were seven other couples going through it at the same time. I ran through it quickly, only glancing to see if it was adequate. It seemed clean so I grabbed the children, Brad, and Amy and ran them out to the car. "Get me to your house!" I told my brother. "I want to call the owner and tell him I want the place!"

Unfortunately, when I spoke to the owner, Mr. Larsen, to say I wanted to rent the townhome, he laughed and said, "Only you and everybody else! I am taking credit information from everyone to run credit reports, and I will let you know."

I gave him the information he requested, reiterated how badly I wanted it, and asked him to please give me a chance.

I went to bed worrying all over again. I thought about all the other couples who wanted the townhome too. *They are married and probably have two incomes,* I thought. *They are probably already established in their jobs and not starting out with a new job in a new area without a spouse to help out financially.* I was mentally beating myself up and driving myself into the ground with all the reasons why I was not good enough to be the one to get the townhome.

Feelings of discouragement flooded my heart, and my deepest fears began to surface. Then suddenly, flashes of the morning at my mother's house, when I was going down the stairs and crying about being homeless, overcame those other thoughts. I remembered the family Bible and God telling me he had prepared a place for us. A peace settled over me, and I cried out to God, "That's it! If the townhome is what you planned for us, God, then it will work out. And if it's not, then you must have another place waiting."

As I closed my eyes, I realized I was experiencing a new attitude, I found myself choosing to trust God instead of allowing myself to be swallowed up in fear and doubt. I rested my head on the pillow, reminding myself of God's promise, and I slowly drifted off to sleep.

The trust in God I experienced was also infusing courage and perseverance within me. I persistently called Mr. Larsen the next two days to see if he had made a decision yet. The answer was always the same: "Not yet." Finally, on the third day, he answered, "Wendy, I ran everyone's credit report, and it looks like out of all the inquires, and based on your credit score, you have the least chance of defaulting on your rent. So since you were the first to ask and have been calling me constantly, if you want it, it's yours."

His words about my credit score caused a flashback to the financial nightmare I had just been through. If it were not for God's help and the sale of the house, along with the help of my friends who quickly assisted me with the unloading of the majority of my financial liabilities, I would never have been able to keep my credit score clean.

"I want it! I want it!" I cried. "Thank you so much Mr. Larsen. Thank you so much!"

"Well," Mr. Larsen said, seemingly with a smile in his voice, "since I have you on the telephone, let's go ahead and complete the application." He went through it line by line, asking questions and waiting for my answers. Then he asked,

"Do you have a dog?" His question surprised me and it made me jump inside.

I slowly answered, "No ... my daughter would like one, but I told her we would have to see if it was allowed."

"Every kid needs a dog!" Mr. Larsen exclaimed. "I'll put dog on the lease. You don't have to pay any extra deposit for a dog."

I was stunned! I couldn't believe what I was hearing! I had never heard of a landlord telling his tenant to get a dog and put it in his rental! There was no doubt in my heart or mind that this townhome and Mr. Larsen were truly a miracle and gift from God, most specifically for my daughter. It was as if God was reaching down from heaven and placing a specially wrapped package, filled with love and compassion, directly on the doorstep for Emily.

Mr. Larsen said the current tenants would be in the townhome through most of November, but I should be able to move in by Thanksgiving.

The townhome had everything on our list, even a dog! I was so excited to tell the children and my mother the good news. And it was only a matter of minutes before I was calling Brad and Amy as well, along with other family members who had been hoping and praying for us. "We have so much to celebrate!" I said, and I quickly reminded everyone of the promise I had received from God back in July that he was preparing a place for us.

God is so big, all-knowing, and powerful, I thought. It was apparent that God was ever faithful in keeping his word to me, unlike any other relationship I had experienced in my past. For the first time in my life, I felt there was someone in whom I could truly trust, rely, and believe—someone who loved me and accepted me and who would watch over and care for me. Someone who would not let me down. The realization caused me to cry out, "Oh, God! I am so sorry I chose to live my life without you for so long!" Now that I had felt his love, his compassion, his comfort, and his provision, I could never again live my life without God. I am ever grateful and changed forever.

Chapter 12

The Oval Tub

My new job started on November 1, but we would not be able to move into the townhome until late November. Brad and Amy graciously invited the children and me to move into their home toward the end of October and stay for the interim. We gladly accepted their offer. After thanking my mother for her loving care and for taking us into her home, we went off on our new adventure.

What I didn't know ahead of time but immediately discovered was how wonderfully important it would be for us to spend time with Brad and Amy before venturing out on our own. I was still fragile, frightened, and didn't want to be alone. This timing must have been part of God's plan in transitioning us into a new life. Brad ignited a fire in us to get outside and do things, like go to the beach, go snorkeling, and play Frisbee. Amy was our comforter. She spent many hours compassionately listening, praying, and encouraging us.

Amy also helped me find a new physician and counselors in the area, so the children and I could continue the long stretch of healing that lay ahead. I specifically requested counselors who were Christian-based, and the Lord honored that request with wonderful support. We were also blessed with an amazing school counselor, Mrs. Griffin, who, upon registering the children for school, met with us and personally committed herself to helping us in any way she could during the very difficult transitional days that lay ahead. We informed her of the unknown number of future trips ahead of us, due to subpoenas and legal hearings.

As much as I could see God's hand over us, the constant retelling of our story to each new person along the way wore us down emotionally, mentally, and physically—so much so that by the time I started my new job, both Emily and I had become ill. For a few weeks, we took turns running high fevers and suffering from colds, sore throats, and sinus infections. It was apparent that the stress and anxiety were wearing us down and attacking our immune systems.

Since Emily and I shared the pull-out couch in Brad and Amy's den, we mastered a way of caring for each other. I would stroke her brow and run my fingers through her hair when she needed comfort, and she would read me the Sermon on the Mount from the Bible (Matthew 5–7) when I needed comfort. I cannot begin to tell you how many times I begged her to read it to me. Sometimes she would respond with "Again?"—and then we would laugh as I said, "Oh yes, please read it again. I can't remember what it said."

I felt as if the Scriptures were talking directly to me as she read through the Beatitudes. There were words that spoke of loving your enemies and praying for those who persecute you and cause you pain. It would take time for me to grasp such a concept, yet I was willing to be taught, because I was learning to trust in the words of this God who was loving me so deeply.

One of the first things Amy asked after we moved in was if I would like to go to church with her. "Amy, I haven't gone to church in eighteen years," I told her. "I swore I would never walk into another church again for the rest of my life, but yes, I really want to go with you."

As we entered the church, two gracious women, Paula and Theresa, immediately greeted me. They must have recognized my new face and paid special attention, making sure I felt welcome. Their friendly smiles and warm spirits were just what I needed to break the ice. Walking into a church defied the promise I had made to myself years earlier, and for me, this step was a huge leap of faith.

The service began with worship music, and the words to the songs brought comfort and tears to my broken heart. Then, it was as if the pastor's message had been prepared specifically for me that day. Over and over again I heard about the love of my heavenly Father, I heard about promises of hope, assurance, acceptance, and God's unfailing and ever-faithful love for me. The message brought healing to my soul and described the God I had already begun to know personally. *You mean others are experiencing the same amazing love from God that I am?* I wondered. My heart felt safe, and I didn't want to leave. I wished I could sit there in church, twenty-four hours a day, seven days a week.

The change that came over me astonished me. When I'd decided to never go to church again, I had seen God and the church (the people and the building) as one. I thought that if someone went to church, it meant that person was perfect— or at least trying to be. That image was crushed when my life was so traumatically damaged by someone who attended church and who, after hurting me, stood so boldly in the congregation. I no longer felt safe and definitely didn't trust anything about church or the people who attended. I had refused to acknowledge God in my life since that time. Now, as I looked around the room, I realized it was filled with all kinds of people who came from all walks of life. It dawned on me that not only was it true that nobody was perfect, but each person attending could be there for a number of different reasons. And perhaps some of them were just like me—very broken.

It's not the building or the people in whom I should be putting my trust, I thought, *but the God who has called us together, who offers a place of healing, a place to worship, a place of fellowship, and a place to encourage and pray for one another.* I was beginning to see myself surrounded with truth—the truth that was promised to me in the backseat of my mother's car when I pulled out my little Bible and read: "To the elect [chosen] lady and her children, whom I love in truth, and not only I, but also all those who have known the truth, because of the truth which abides in us and will be with us forever: Grace, mercy, and peace will be with you from God the Father and from the Lord Jesus Christ, the Son of the Father, in truth and love" (2 John 1:1–3 NKJV).

The Word of God was truth, and hearing the messages that seemed to speak directly to me, week after week, slowly assisted my heart and soul in being set free.

I could not start a workday or even enter the office building of my new job without first saying a prayer and reading Psalm 23. The world was a frightening place to me. I may have looked calm and collected on the outside, but on the inside I was shattered, I was nervous, and I was fearful. I wondered if I would be able to remember what to do or how to do it once I sat at my desk. Psalm 23 was a comforting reminder to me, each new day, that the Lord was with me, that he would shield me, and that he would care for me and comfort me, no matter what kind of frightening environment lay before me. Yes, this is what I wanted—his goodness and love to be with me all the days of my life.

> *The Lord is my shepherd, I lack nothing. He makes me lie down in green pastures, he leads me beside quiet waters, he refreshes my soul. He guides me along the right paths for his name's sake. Even though I walk through the darkest valley, I will fear no evil, for you are with me; your rod and your staff, they comfort me. You prepare a table before me in the presence of my enemies. You anoint my head with oil; my cup overflows. Surely your goodness and love will follow me all the days of my life, and I will dwell in the house of the Lord forever. —Psalm 23 (NIV)*

Thanksgiving was quickly approaching, and oh, how appropriate. Our move fell on Thanksgiving weekend. We had so much to be thankful for and a new home was such a miraculous blessing. "How incredible God is!" I told Amy. "He never stops amazing me. It was on Independence Day that we were set free, and now a beautiful, bountiful blessing—a new home—on Thanksgiving Day."

It was so exciting to think that we would be on our own again, yet deep inside I was frightened to be on my own. I relied heavily on the encouragement and strength of my family. I had been emotionally and mentally spoon-fed by my mother and then by Brad and Amy. Stepping out on my own was more like learning to walk again after being wheelchair-bound for a very long time. *Baby steps*, I thought, *baby steps*.

Brad was extremely supportive, and he took the trip north with the children and me as we drove back to pick up our things from storage. We were greeted by friends upon our arrival, and with all the assistance, it didn't take long before the moving van was filled to the brim. It was strange seeing our things after all these months, yet the familiarity was like running into long-lost friends. It was amazing to realize how well we'd gotten by on so little.

We said our last farewells to our friends, and as my brother was rolling down the back door of the moving van, a new fear struck me. What if once we put our furniture into the new house, it looked or felt like our old house? What if it brought back terrible memories for all of us, most especially for Emily? As we climbed into the cab, I closed my eyes and said a little prayer within my heart. I asked God to please help us out in this situation, for I did not have the funds to refurnish our house. These were the only belongings we had and all we could use to set up our home.

We returned to Brad and Amy's home late that night, and early the next morning, I contacted the landlord to get our house key. It had been weeks since we'd first seen the townhome, and then it had been for only a brief moment as I ran up and down the stairs—I'd been in a rush to call the landlord to tell him we wanted this place.

Now, as we walked toward the front door with key in hand, I was once again overwhelmed with gratitude for the gift of this home. It had everything on our list, and now it was ours. God had been faithful, and we had been blessed.

Much to my surprise, as I entered my new master bedroom and bath, I noticed for the first time that there was an oval tub. My knees buckled, and I burst into tears as flashbacks of one of my last conversations with Lawrence was asking specifically if we could have an oval tub in our new home. I remember him looking back at me and replying, "We'll see," and then he drove away that Sunday afternoon, the day before he was arrested.

When I wrote the list of items we needed in a home, those things I was hoping and praying for, I'd listed only the ones that my children needed or that would reduce our financial cost. An oval tub had been something I had missed in our prior home, and I had begged to have another one when we relocated near the academy.

But I hadn't added an oval tub—my own heart's desire and a place I ran to for warmth and comfort—to the list of things the children and I needed in a home. Shock and amazement overwhelmed me as I realized that not only had God honored our list of requests, but he also honored a desire that I had kept locked secretly away, deep within my heart. Now more than ever, I needed to know this God who so intimately knew and loved me. Yes, once again I felt a yearning and wanting more than ever before to learn how to love him back.

Another one of my fears was eliminated when we brought our furniture into the home, where the color tones—bright whites and blues instead of the earth tones in our old place— made our furniture look brand new. I later found out the townhome had been painted and new carpet laid at just about the same time I'd read the words from our family Bible: "Let not your heart be troubled," followed by "I go to prepare a place for you," and "if it were not so, I would have told you" (John 14:1-2 KJV). Yes, the townhome's colors had been changed; God literally meant what he said when he told me he was preparing a place just for us!

I will never forget one particularly bright and sunny morning, shortly after moving in, while I was driving out of our townhome complex on my way to work. I caught a glimpse of our townhome in my rearview mirror and was instantly overwhelmed with gratitude and taken aback by the sight—so much so that I had to pull over before exiting the driveway. There it was, our townhome, nestled so gracefully in the trees beyond the beautifully landscaped grounds and pool area. I called out in my car, "God, why are you so good to me?" I knew full well that I had done nothing to deserve such great love and care. I heard a loud voice in my head instantaneously reply, "Wendy, there will be days when you will wonder if I am really here, and you will remember this and know that I *am!*"

I sat there, speechless. God was no longer only a possibility or a figment of my imagination. No, God was real, and I knew! The touch of his Holy Spirit that I had felt earlier and the ongoing reinforcement of his love definitely told me that my God was for me and not against me. I realized that even more, my God was and is the great "I AM." He was telling me, "I *am* real," "I *am* here," and "I *am* always a choice!"

Graciously, God was also forewarning me that there would be days when I would wonder if he was really there, which meant there would be more challenges ahead. *Only next time, I thought, I will know that I am not alone and that I can trust in a God who promises to be with me all the way, through any circumstance I face, encouraging me to have faith.* This promise to me was like God's laying down stepping stones, placing them in a straight line. He promised he would provide a path for me and that he would make a way for me, no matter what the situation looked like, if only I would ask, if only I would choose, and if only I would trust him.

I also discovered that the true joy of finding a home wasn't just about the physical walls of a townhome but the spiritual walls of my heart. I was learning that my heart was a place God knew intimately. And it was a place that, if I invited him, God would also reside. Opening my heart to God opened up an entirely new world for me. As I chose to allow God to be in control, I also invited him to lead me, guide me, and fulfill his promises in me. I allowed this loving God to care for us, comfort us, love us, and provide a layer of protection and covering over us. This was something that I am now convinced is exactly what he has always wanted to do. He just needed me to say yes.

> *"I have been standing at the door, and I am constantly knocking. If anyone hears me calling him and opens the door, I will come in and fellowship with him and he with me"—Revelations 3:20 (LB)*

Chapter 13

Riviera

Shortly after moving into our new home, I received a message from the Victim Witness Program. Their staff had voted the children and me Family of the Year for the county, and each employee personally donated funds to provide a Christmas gift for us, which were gift certificates to a large variety store in our local area. Their act of kindness brought tears to my eyes, as funds were tight—we were living from one paycheck to another. Once again, God was letting me know he was watching over us, and everything was going to get better because he was the one taking care of us now.

The Christmas season came with a mix of emotions for the children and me—some of loss but others of hope. For the first time, I truly listened to the Christmas story and the birth of Jesus Christ. I personally gave thanks to my Lord for coming to earth, paying the price for my sins on the cross, and rising again.

The holiday season also told me it was time to start looking for a dog for Emily, so to get the ball rolling, I surprised her with dog-related Christmas gifts: a dog bed, dog toys, dog brush, and a leash. "It is time to start looking!" I told Emily as we laughed at the gifts she found under the tree.

Amy took Emily to a few different dog shelters in the area while I was at work. Emily also visited additional shelters with different family members but to no avail. She could not find the perfect dog for her. Finally, one cold and rainy Sunday morning, Emily asked me if I would take her to the shelters to look yet another time.

"Sure, sweetheart," I answered, "we can go right after church." When I got home, I looked at the long list of dog shelters, leaned over the edge of my oval tub, and began to pray. "Lord, thank you for giving us a home that will allow us to have a dog. Because of this miracle, I know you want Emily to have one. So Lord, will you please help us find that special dog, the one you have picked out especially for her, the one that will bring her lots of love, comfort, and joy."

Emily had mentioned wanting to go to the shelters at the northern end of the county, but when I looked at the list again after praying and asking God to direct us, the animal shelter at the very southern end of the county seemed to pop off the page at me, inspiring me to head south instead.

The winds were strong that Sunday afternoon, and the raindrops must have been coming directly from the animal shelter itself, for they were as large as cats and dogs! I found myself more lost after every turn of the road through the rolling hills. Finally, I saw a pay phone up ahead and quickly pulled over. I grabbed some coins from my purse, opened my umbrella, and leapt out of the car and into the storm toward the pay phone. The wind kept trying to turn the telephone book pages for me, and my umbrella made several attempts to fly away. In spite of the weather, I found the listing, but as I asked the shelter's receptionist for directions, the wind blew my umbrella completely inside out!

We were lost, we were cold, and I was drenched, but I was not going to give up. I glanced back toward the car and saw a surprised look on Emily's face. Between the look on her face and the hope that sprang up within me, I laughed in the midst of this storm. I knew God had opened the door for Emily to have a dog, and I knew he was leading me to the right shelter, so all I could do was persevere, exercise faith, and keep going. Shortly after getting the additional directions from the shelter, we were finally able to locate it.

As the animal shelter's personnel walked us up and down the kennel aisles, all the dogs began barking wildly, jumping up on their hind legs, and pawing their cage walls—that is, all but one big black dog that sat quietly looking up at us. One ear stood straight up and the other one flopped down. She was a black Lab/Chow mix. Her nametag on the fence said "Riviera," and it was love at first sight for my daughter. "She's a big dog!" I exclaimed as we stopped to notice how different she was from all the rest.

"I want big!" Emily replied. "I want one so big I can hug her and lay on her and play with her!"

Within a few minutes, we were back in the office, completing the paperwork. It would take one week to process the papers, they told us, and if everything checked out okay, she would be ours. One of the shelter's first requirements was verification from our landlord, confirming his approval for us to have a dog. This requirement surprised me, but God already knew and had this one covered!

One week later, we were a family of four—a mom, her two children, and a dog. Emily was in heaven with her newfound friend, and I decided we required a new family portrait. We went to a studio down the street and decided to have a white background so the dark-haired dog would show up in the photo. I will never forget the day I gave the new portrait to my father to replace the old one that had once hung on the family photo wall in his house. "Dad, you will always be able to hang this picture on the wall, even if the dog runs away or is no longer with us some day!" What I said made us laugh, but deep inside and behind the smile was a sadness, a sorrow, and a history of past disappointments.

The weeks ahead were filled with numerous challenges, and Riviera's playful and protective disposition was a helpful distraction—although we could have done without the skunk-chasing incidents and tomato-juice baths! Weekdays consisted of counseling and doctor appointments in between work hours and school. Intermittent emotional breakdowns occurred within each of us along the way. It was astonishing to see how quickly the slightest thing could set off our emotions, rapidly reminding us of our pain and constantly reopening our wounds.

As an example, and in an attempt to make light of a difficult situation, whenever Emily and I were together and saw an officer of the law or a police car go by, we'd immediately turn, look at each other, draw our hands in front of our faces, and, with outstretched fingers like a cat, make the sound of a cat going "R-r-r-r-r." Our actions were not meant to disrespect the law, but in some silly way, we were trying to dilute the pain that each sighting brought to mind. On the other hand, when I was alone, I was more prone to turn away quickly, because truthfully, the sight ignited a fiery dagger that pierced my heart, reminding me of the lies, the loss, and the pain all over again.

Another thing that set off overwhelming emotions was seeing stories about others' misfortunes on the television and in the newspaper. It was apparent that my experiences had distorted my view, causing me to see the media and their grasp at another story as a type of predatory behavior, as they appeared to use people's pain and loss for their own gain and ratings. Watching them in action only reminded me of our own front-page headlines and the camera crew I found standing at my front door and walking through my neighborhood. I was reminded of the reasons why we needed to protect ourselves and run for safety. So in my attempt at survival, I refused to watch television, read the newspaper, or associate in any way with the news media.

Even songs on the radio turned me upside down. They would quickly remind me of a life I had always wanted, as well as the reality in which all my dreams had been so violently crushed. Love songs especially ripped my heart out, and the only way I could get through being in a place where such songs were played was to replace the person of love or the hero in the song with thoughts of my own true Savior, Jesus Christ, rather than thinking of the men in my life who had always let me down.

As time went on, I realized that the oval tub became my hiding place, my prayer closet, and my tranquil getaway to praise, pray, and ponder. I spent many nights before bed, unwinding in the bubbles and washing away the tears from my face. I never knew when we moved into our townhome just how much I would need that oval tub to assist in my own healing.

The healing process was taking much longer than I had hoped. We were all dealing with our own issues, and the pain we each experienced was triggered by different circumstances. As I tried to deal with my own hurt, I found that each new trigger not only reminded me of my current pain but also brought up pain from past situations which were similar in nature or emotion. Instead of one catastrophe, it felt like a dozen devastations all at once, one heaped on top of the other. It was a constant battle with overwhelming feelings of fear and loss, discouragement and depression, or rejection and abandonment that would flood me without warning. The redeeming news was that I was learning that everything I was going through, Jesus had already been through and had conquered. I knew Jesus had the answer, and he was the hope I wanted to hold on to.

The children and I were not the only ones to require healing in our home. It was evident Riviera needed a chance to feel safe and secure as well. "Look how Riviera hunkers down and runs out of the room every time I walk in with a brush or a broom in my hand," I mentioned to Emily. It was apparent this seventy-pound dog also had been abused. The shelter told us she had been found in a public restroom, tied to a pipe. It was so hard to believe this loyal, dedicated, well-behaved, loving, playful, and protective dog had been abused and abandoned. Ultimately, Riviera was just what my daughter needed, and Emily was definitely what Riviera needed too. God sure has a wonderful way of answering our prayers for help and taking care of everyone's needs all at once.

Riviera was just one of the first steps in bringing healing into our home. The next thing on the list was to fill our walls and rooms with words of truth and the promises of God. I couldn't afford much, but I found some greeting cards with encouraging sayings and words of hope, and I framed them and put them on the hallway wall and in all the bathrooms. I also placed a printout on the refrigerator of Isaiah 40:28–31, which was perfect, because we needed all the help we could get to increase our faith and remind us that life can be better.

Do you not know? Have you not heard? The Lord is the everlasting God, the Creator of the ends of the earth. He will not grow tired or weary, and his understanding no one can fathom. He gives strength to the weary and increases the power of the weak, and young men stumble and fall; but those who hope in the Lord will renew their strength. They will soar on wings like eagles; they will run and not grow weary, they will walk and not be faint. (Isaiah 40:28-31 NIV)

There was one picture I went out on a limb to buy, and it meant the most to me. It was a picture of a little girl and her younger brother, walking across a broken-down bridge with an angel right beside them, gently guiding them across in safety. I hung it on the wall at the top of the stairs where each one of us could not help but see it as we walked up to the second level, where all our bedrooms were located. It was a daily reminder and prayer in my heart, asking God to please watch over my children and help them get through each new day.

And just as I filled the house with pictures and sayings of inspiration, I chose only to listen to encouraging Christian music when I was by myself—music that fed my heart and soul with encouragement, hope, and reminders of God's love for me. Whether I was in my bath, in my car, or getting ready for work in the morning, I flooded my life with God's love and truth. I did all I could do to stay in an emotionally safe and uplifting place, for life was continually throwing me curveballs and knocking me to the ground. I needed to fill my fears with faith, my pain with hope, and my heart with trust. By choosing to feed on God's words and promises through music, I was encouraged by his power and strength, which was just what I needed for the challenging days and weeks that lay ahead.

Then there were the counseling sessions, which would be an ongoing process. Healing, I found, was a lot like an onion—each breakthrough only seemed to expose another layer right below the last. And one thing was for sure: after studying and discussing with the counselor the long-term effects of the crimes that were committed, more than anything I longed for transparency in and around my children and me. I was also extremely concerned for the choices my children—and most especially Emily—would make going forward. Would she rise above this? Or would she believe the lies that might be telling her everything was lost? I had heard of victims who did not heal from their abuse and instead led their lives as if the secrets and the unmerited shame or embarrassment somehow defined who they were.

It was this specific fear that initiated constant prayer and continual concern in me for Emily. And I had an entirely different list of concerns and prayers for Christopher. My ongoing request to Amy every time we got together was "Will you pray with me for my children?" Also, going up to the front of the sanctuary at the end of a church service for prayer became a weekly event. We had so many challenges ahead of us, like learning to identify our fears and make healthy life choices, and dealing with betrayal, abandonment, and father issues, just to name a few.

While driving Emily home from a counseling appointment one day, I felt an urge to talk to her about my concern. "You are at a crossroads," I said. "You could take one of two directions. I've seen people destroy themselves with alcohol and drugs, sleeping around, never quite knowing where they are going to wake up, because they believed a lie that told them that's all they could be now, because they were marked, marred, or tainted." Then I mentioned someone we both knew and the sad choices we had watched that person make. "But I have also seen victims get help, rise above the pain, choose to walk with integrity, and care about others around them," I said. "I have seen them become the biggest defender of truth, a voice and an advocate for the abused. This is what I want. I want you to choose the healthy road. I want you to rise above this. Let's not let the predator win. Instead, use it to expose the truth and help others find a way out of it too."

I had heard other Christians talking about Romans 8:28 as well as other Scriptures that referred to the power and ability of God to turn evil or destructive situations into a positive force for good, and I shared them with Emily. "This is exactly what I want for our lives now," I said as we contemplated the pain and anguish we had been through. Just as God heard my cry and turned our world from a place of total loss to a place of hope—with a new home and a dog—I wanted our lives to rise above the muck and the mire, rather than being swallowed up by it.

It was at that very moment, sitting in our car, that Emily and I made a promise to each other. We promised from that day forward we would not let this pain be in vain. We would rise above it, and we would ask God to turn it for good, hoping that somehow God would also use us to help others find hope.

Chapter 14

On My Knees

The children and I were beginning to adjust to the new routine at home, but facing the world was another story. Each one of us had our own particular challenges, and the workplace was one of mine. As tough as it was, I could never begin to express how extremely grateful I was to have a job—especially one so close to home. It was a miracle I found a position so quickly. More than anything, I was so thankful for the chance to have the children's lives finally begin to settle down by having a permanent home, a good school, an amazing dog, and a loving family close by.

Adjusting to a new position always takes time, but there were additional challenges which left me on edge. The company had been in business for some time, but the longest any of the current personnel had been working for the owners was three months. Within the first few weeks of employment, I began to understand some of the reasons for this oddity.

Shortly after starting my job, fear swept through me as I overheard an employee and her spouse yelling to someone in the administration's office. They were complaining about her paycheck bouncing for the second time. I had no savings and was totally dependent on my paycheck to cover my rent and take care of my children. I quickly bowed my head in prayer right then and there at my desk, asking God for his protection, direction, and provision.

"What should I do?" I whispered to God in desperation. Just as quickly as I put the question to God, I sensed him giving me directions. *"When you receive your first paycheck, take it directly to the company's bank as listed on the check and cash it there. Do this each and every payday on your lunch break."* I knew the answer was coming from God because an inner blanket of peace started to tame the fear and anxiety that had been making it difficult for me to breathe.

In the days that followed, I continued with the same routine and used my lunch hour to go to the company's bank and cash my paycheck. Then, at the end of each of those workdays, I would visit my own bank and deposit the cash into my account. Payday after payday, each check was cashed without fail, and after every deposit I gave thanks to the Lord for his guidance and loving provision.

Employee complaints regarding paychecks bouncing became more widespread throughout the company. I found myself answering telephone calls from people who threatened to shut off the utilities and lock the front doors of our building. But amazingly—and undoubtedly with the help of God's hand—my department's success rate skyrocketed astronomically, and the company's financial burden began to lift.

By the end of my second month of employment, we had collected over 200 percent of that month's generated revenue, due to the aged accounts receivable we were able to recover. We were also able to verify our recovery of funds on the rest of the outstanding balances that would be coming in within the next few weeks. We had quickly cleaned up a mess that had taken months to make.

With all the outstanding accounts collected, I thought the financial problems would soon be over, but instead, the complaints and calls continued. As a matter of fact, things got much worse.

"Wendy, why is the amount on my paycheck getting smaller and smaller every pay period, even though I am working the same number of hours?" asked Sarah, an employee I oversaw and a main contributor to our department's success.

"I don't know," I answered. "Let me run upstairs and look over your time cards."

As I opened the filing cabinet and glanced over her time cards, I could see someone had been crossing out the total number of punched-in hours and writing in a progressively smaller number of hours on each consecutive time card.

I took the stack of time cards and headed to the administration's office in an urgent attempt to share the employee's question and my newfound concern.

"It's because we can't afford to pay any more hours than that!" came a surprisingly snappy reply.

"Then," I answered, "we need to have her work fewer hours."

With that, the woman picked up the telephone receiver and shoved it toward me, saying "You take these calls from the utility companies and tell them why we can't pay their bills!" Without saying a word, I asked the Lord for his strength, his insight, and his help. I needed the Lord's strength and power to help me through this terribly frightening situation. I stood tall, but I did not feel led to speak, so I kept quiet, while thoughts of the numerous lies and deceit from which my children and I had fled resurfaced in my mind.

As I stood there in silence, and while the ranting and raving of things beyond my control continued, I found myself looking to the Lord for his reassurance and quickly remembered his promise that he would never leave me or forsake me.

"There will be days," the Lord had warned me, *"when you will wonder if I am really here, and you will remember this and know that I AM."*

The words that the Lord had given me just a few months earlier quickly flooded my mind and were backed by numerous memories of his miraculous interventions. I looked up toward the heavens as bits and pieces of the Scriptures began filling my thoughts. They were promises that confirmed God's love for me. They were reminders that if I sought the Lord, I would find him, and if I asked the Lord to be my refuge, he would also be my pillar of strength. God's promises were like knots in a rope for me now, providing something tangible to hang on to, even when everything else around me felt as if it was trying to emotionally pull me to the ground.

Eventually, although without resolution, I was excused and allowed to return to my department. By this time, it was approaching five o'clock. *Thank goodness*, I thought as I grabbed my purse and prepared to leave. I stopped to take a deep breath, noticing that once again, fear and anxiety were trying to rear their ugly heads.

"Wendy, are you all right?" asked Sarah, who was cleaning up her desk for the day.

"Yes, yes, I'm fine. Our concern is not resolved, but I need to leave now," I explained. I closed my eyes for a brief moment, trying desperately to pull myself together. "It's Valentine's Day, so I'm volunteering at my church this evening. I've offered to babysit so parents without childcare can still go out and enjoy a romantic night together. I truly believe in marriage, and I cannot think of a better way to get past my own loneliness than to focus on another's needs instead of dwelling on the fact that I don't have a partner myself."

As I turned to head toward the door, one of the administration team walked in. "Wendy," she said quickly, "I need you to come back upstairs. We have to talk to you."

"Okay," I answered, "but I have a commitment to be somewhere in a half hour." My heart was racing, and my anxiety level increased as we walked down the hall in silence.

"Wendy, we need you to sit down at this computer!" A hand popped out in front of me, pointing toward the chair in front of the computer. I hesitantly sat down, watching while multiple spreadsheets and numerous columns rolled past on the screen.

"I am not sure what this is or what it means," I said after viewing worksheet after worksheet of what seemed to be completely unassociated with our business.

"This is our budget," one of the administration team member's shrieked. "This is why we had to pay less on the time cards. And Wendy, this is why you have to bring in a whole lot more money!"

I sat there for over two hours as she drilled me with questions and insisted that we needed more money. I tried to excuse myself once, but the administration team refused to let me leave and only began yelling at me even more. "We need you to bring in three times the collections that you just brought in. You need to bring in more money!"

My mind went blank, and all I could do was cry out to the Lord in my heart, ask God to help me with a healthy response, and hopefully quiet their angry words. Slowly, without thought, words began flowing through my lips. "My department has made incredible strides in collecting and cleaning up the outstanding accounts receivable," I said, "but I cannot collect more than the actual charges the company generates."

The statement quieted their outburst, but it was apparent my words were not what they wanted to hear.

By the time I left the office and got to my car, I realized I was overwhelmed with fear and paralyzed by shock once again. "Oh God, help me, help me, please!" I cried as I drove in the direction of the church.

I quickly ran into the church's foyer, apologizing for not being there earlier to babysit. With tears running down my face, I quickly turned to leave.

"Are you okay? Can we pray for you?" asked one of the ladies behind the counter.

"Oh yes, yes, please pray for me," I cried as I pushed the door open to leave. "It's been a terribly difficult day at work. I am so sorry, but I cannot stay."

It had only been seven and a half months since my entire world had been turned upside down and pulled out from under me. My courage and strength had been growing, but I was still fragile, so much so that the very thought of being linked to anything unethical or unjust in any way threw me whirling into what felt like the beginning of another emotional breakdown. I wanted desperately to feel safe again, and as I sat in my car, weeping hysterically, I cried out, "What do I do now? Where do I go? I need help, dear Lord God! I need help! I am crashing! I am crashing! Please help me, Lord. *Please* help me, Lord!"

With my head leaning against the steering wheel and tears running down my cheeks, the image of my family doctor's face flashed through my mind. Then, a small still voice in my head said, *"Go directly to your doctor's office."* Without hesitation and in total panic, I drove straight to her office, swiping at the tears so I could see where I was driving. As it turned out, my doctor worked until eight o'clock two nights a week, and this was one of her late nights.

My family doctor was known for her compassionate nature, and she had played an instrumental role in the health care of my children and me after we moved into town. She was also aware of our story. As I lay on my side, huddled in a fetal position on her exam table, she had a clear understanding of why I was crying. I was desperately trying to survive in a world that kept reopening my wounds.

It didn't take long before the doctor convinced me I should not return to my workplace but instead find another job. "It's not a healthy environment for you, Wendy," she insisted. "Besides, you have an impeccable work ethic and a remarkable track record. You will find a better job." The doctor's voice was stern, yet she kept a gentle smile, and the kind look in her eyes told me somehow she knew it would all work out.

As overwhelmed as I was, there was a newfound hope deep within me. In my past life, I would have already decided that all was lost and would have given up. And in the depths of my despair, I may have even succumbed to suicidal thoughts at the very idea that life was more than I could handle. Yet now, as I recalled the past seven and a half months and the remarkable love, compassion, guidance, and merciful direction I had experienced from the Lord, I realized something had changed in me. It was a confidence and a hope in God and in his loving kindness that had made all the difference.

"Wendy, I want you to come down and visit me this weekend," my mother suggested when I called to let her know that I needed to find a new job. "Your sister and brother-in-law are coming down from up north to lead worship music at my seminar, and I want you to come too." An encouraging weekend with family was just what the doctor ordered, and I was happily surprised to find out that my niece, Loni, was going to be singing also. She was only one month older than Emily and had the voice of an angel.

With all of her heart, Loni sang the beautiful words of "On My Knees" by Jaci Velasquez. As each passionate word rang out, it dove deeper into my soul. I sat there silently as tears streamed down my cheeks, listening to her sing words about it not mattering whether in laughter or in pain; the only way to survive was "on my knees."

Loni's singing words of encouragement and hope inspired me to listen to more worship songs throughout the day. And I made sure to read a daily devotional each morning in my prayer time. *Our Daily Bread* (a publication by RBC Ministries in Grand Rapids, Michigan) and *365 Day Brighteners for God's Word—Promises and Blessings from Scripture* (published by Garborg's, a brand of Day Spring Cards, Inc.) were among my first favorites. Each page overflowed with uplifting promises from the Word of God, igniting my heart and filling me with hope.

Saturating my life with God's unfailing truth launched both my spiritual and emotional health toward recovery. In addition to the Bible, one of the most life-changing and faith-inspiring books I read was *Prison to Praise* by Merlin Carothers. His true-life story inspired me. His faith in God encouraged me. And the trusting and grateful heart he chose to have, no matter what the circumstances he encountered, taught me more about applying faith, courage, and perseverance into my life. *This*, I thought, *is exactly what I need to pursue another job.*

Merlin's book begins by quoting Scripture: "Rejoice always, pray continually, give thanks in all circumstances;

for this is God's will for you in Christ Jesus" (1 Thessalonians 5:16–18 NIV). Merlin's true-life experience was not just about a physical prison but a prison of circumstances and how he personally learned to choose faith over fear. His words were inspiring, and the truth he shared about how faith, trust, and gratitude changed his life forever also set my heart on fire to walk in these same ways and know the Lord even deeper.

I could not put the book down until I had read the entire thing. There were a couple of statements that popped right off the page at me and helped me to understand the truth about faith much more clearly. On page 42 of *Prison to Praise*, Merlin Carothers writes: "Trusting God apparently meant going out on a limb without anything to hold onto but faith."

I began to understand that this concept of walking by faith was a lot like walking with a blindfold. I could not see what was ahead, but based on the God I was getting to know, I had to trust that he would work things out for my good. Then on page 85, I saw: "[Wendy, if] you can only believe that God is really working this thing out for the best ... then all you have to do is trust him and begin to thank him regardless of what the situation looks like."

"Trust and gratitude," I said out loud as I stopped to ponder for a moment. *If I am going to ask God to be in control of my life*, I thought, *then a thankful heart is definitely in order, not only for the things I can see God doing but also for the things I cannot. After all, isn't this what I have learned over the past months by watching God move through my children's and my lives? Haven't I already experienced God making a way where there seemed to be no way?* "Now is not the time to give up, Wendy!" I said to myself.

I had to admit it: I had done more than my share of worrying and complaining, even after being amazed by one miracle after another as I watched God work things out in my life. *Yes, it all makes sense,* I thought. Now if I could only remember to focus on trusting, listening, and heeding God's promptings and thanking him for his hand over my life, instead of what I usually did, which was put all my focus on what seemed to be going wrong!

"Okay, Lord," I said aloud, "I am going to start trusting you, and I am going to start thanking you for your help, even for the answers I cannot see yet. I know my faith is a bit shaky, so will you please fill me up with that too? Based on the past months, I know you are there, and the Bible says you are the same yesterday, today, and forever. So I am choosing to trust that you are still here with me, that you still hear my voice, and that you will continue to guide and protect me. Thank you, Lord, that you are already working things out for a new job for me, even if I cannot see it yet and even when it does not seem like a possibility. And most of all, Lord, thank you for your kindness. Thank you for loving me."

I was still a bit frightened, but my courage was building, and I prayed for the strength to start searching once again for a new job. "Oh Lord, where do I start?" I whispered as I knelt quietly at the side of my bed. I thought of the company where I originally had planned to interview but had canceled when I accepted the job I'd just left—it had been with a national company, and the available position had been at their regional office. I wondered if they might have any other openings. "I missed out on the management position, but it's a large regional office," I said out loud. "Perhaps they will have something else available."

After finishing my prayer time, I went over to my desk and pulled out all my old job-search paperwork. I also grabbed the list of contacts I had made months earlier. *Well, at least it's a start,* I thought. *Lord, before I pick up the telephone and make a call,*

*I want you to know that I am making a conscious decision right now
to put my trust in you for the outcome, no matter which way it goes.*

I was relieved when someone answered the telephone
instead of getting voice mail and even more relieved when
the woman who answered and identified herself was the
same person I had spoken to four months earlier. I quickly
introduced myself and explained the reason for my call.

"Oh yes," she said, "I remember you, Wendy. We did fill
the position you were seeking, but the person we hired just
gave notice and left. So we actually have the same position
open again."

After briefly explaining that my prior job did not work
out, I asked if she would be willing to let me come in for an
interview.

"If I recall correctly," the woman responded, "your résumé
did reflect the experience we were seeking. Yes, let's have you
come in for an interview tomorrow, if that works for you. How
does eleven o'clock sound?"

In spite of my nervousness, the interview went very
well, and later that same day I received a phone call and was
offered a position at the company's regional office, which also
included an increase in pay. I joyfully accepted the position.
I was more than grateful to be employed again, yet I found
myself frightened and excited at the same time. But even
more, I was grateful to God for another one of his miracles, as
well as an answered prayer. I was extremely relieved I would
be able to support my children and their needs once again.

Each new day uncovered more new miracles from God,
both big and small. I constantly stood in amazement at his
unfailing love and ever-faithful concern for the children's and
my welfare. The more I remained aware of God's presence and

his love for me, the more I noticed him loving me. "Whatever is good and perfect is a gift coming down to us from God" (James 1:17 NLT). I was noticing that whether through circumstance or another person's words or actions, each new blessing was more than it appeared; it was, in fact, God loving me.

As I thought about God's all-powerful love and kindness, a song came to mind. It had the simplest of words and the catchiest of tunes. It was something I had heard recently at my church home group and was played by the artist himself, Mark Riley, on a ukulele when he visited from the Hawaiian island of Kauai. The words went something like this:

> *Great big things from a great big God,*
> *Great big things from a great big God,*
> *Great big things from a great big God of mercy ...*

My God is a great big God, I thought, and I sang the words over and over again. "This is what I need to always remember, and this is what I must never forget!" I said out loud. The truth is, if I had given up hope after my first position fell apart and not turned to God for help or put my faith and trust in the Lord's hands for the outcome, I may have missed this new employment opportunity with a better salary, and I also would not have learned the most important lesson of all—that my God is bigger than anything or anyone else in this entire world.

> *"He is the one you praise; he is your God, who performed for you those great and awesome wonders you saw with your own eyes" (Deuteronomy 10:21 NIV).*

Chapter 15

Little Lamb

"So how will I break the ice when I meet with my new team at work for the very first time?" I asked myself—and quickly answered, "I know!" I picked up Emily's wire-framed eyeglasses that our dog, Riviera, had chewed up and twisted into a mangled mess just the day before.

After introducing myself to the group as their direct supervisor, I put the glasses on as if to start reading. One by one, each person noticed my looking through the twisted metal without any lenses. The exercise was a success and initiated a lighthearted laugh by all.

Walking into a new setting always made me nervous, but I continued to ask God for his strength and direction with both the workload and the people I supervised. By my sixth month, the team I was leading received companywide recognition for having one of the greatest positive impacts for the quarter. The dedicated teamwork in cleaning up and reducing the average number of accounts usually put on hold for compliance reasons was reduced by 90 percent.

The regional manager exclaimed, "Wendy, how did you do it? I haven't seen a reduction in the hold account's percentage since I've worked here."

"Well, I pray a lot," I responded, "and listen a lot when God answers." I smiled. "It was a pretty big challenge to keep the team motivated and working together. I didn't always know what to do, and in those times I had to rely on my faith in God and his direction to help me through it. You wouldn't believe how many times I had to pray and ask God to help me see what I needed to see or hear what I needed to hear—not to mention the wisdom and strength to actually do something about it."

The manager was quite taken aback by my answer, yet extremely intrigued; he asked a number of new questions. Eventually, I shared my true-life experiences of how God heard my pleas for help, provided a new home for the children and me, and even led us to the perfect dog for my daughter.

"God has helped me through life's circumstances ever since I cried out for help and invited him into my life," I told the manager. "Getting through the difficult circumstances has not always been easy. But I must admit there has never been a time when I've asked God for help that he didn't come through. The answers have not always looked the way I thought they were supposed to, but even in those cases, it always ended up better for everyone involved. Yes, the reason I've made it this far is because God heard my cry for help and is ever so loving and amazingly faithful to answer."

Shortly after the regional meeting took place, I was pleasantly surprised by a familiar voice on the telephone. "Wendy, is that you? This is Bob; remember me?"

"Oh yes, Bob, how are you doing?" Bob and I had worked together at my prior job. We happened to run into each other at the airport just a month earlier when we were both sending family off. At the time, he mentioned that our prior employer still owed him thousands of dollars in back pay. I had given him my phone number and told him to call if he wanted me to speak to the labor board or stand up on his behalf. "Bob, are you calling because you need me to testify for you?" I asked.

"Eventually," Bob responded, "but right now I am calling for another reason." As it turned out, Bob was now working for a company, less than three miles from my home, that was seeking someone with my skills to head up their accounts-receivable department. They'd asked him if he knew of anyone who might qualify. "The company has been around for a number of years," Bob explained, "but they just took on an additional book of business. Funny thing is, I'd just seen an article about your company, and I thought of you. I mentioned you to the owner, and he asked if I would see if you'd be interested in coming in for an interview." Bob assured me the company was stable. "The people are great, and the owner is very reputable, Wendy—unlike our previous experience."

"Oh Bob, I am flattered you would think of me." I said. "Every job has its challenges, and mine surely does too, but things are going pretty well for me here. Although ... the thought of being much closer to home and the children and no longer fighting the bumper-to-bumper traffic on the freeway sounds pretty wonderful." Before we ended our call, however, I told him I would really have to think about it.

"Wow, what an interesting and busy week this has been," I mumbled as I returned to my office after lunch. I was glad to see Friday finally arrive—that is, until I was summoned to the regional manager's office. As I entered the office, I saw one of the company's vice presidents, along with another manager from a different division.

"Wendy, you need to know that your manager has been let go," the vice president said.

"Oh no!" I responded. "What happened?"

The vice president said that a number of branch managers in the region had asked to manage their own accounts. "The corporate office finally agreed to let them do it, but this means additional layoffs. As a matter of fact, I need a list from you of at least four employees you can do without."

I was so grateful for God's timing—my last conversation with my manager had been my own story of hope in starting over. I said a prayer and asked God to please bless him and direct him in his journey. But most of all, I asked God to show my manager just how much God loved him and to make sure he knew that he was not alone.

In the following days, I went though excruciating pain and agony as I contemplated my new assignment. Each time I prayed, thoughts of Bob and our conversation regarding his company came to mind. By the following Monday, there was a much different air in the office, than the week before. *Word must have gotten out*, I thought, as I overheard employees quietly discussing who might go first due to seniority.

Once again, my world was shaken, and I cried out to God in my early morning prayer time, asking, "Why do things have to be so difficult? Why do they have to be so painful, God?" As I closed my eyes in prayer, a scene entered my mind. At the center of the scene, a lamb was walking along, and at its side was a shepherd. The shepherd began tapping on the side of the lamb with his long staff. The lamb abruptly stopped and looked up at the shepherd and said, "Why are you causing me pain?" Then, my view changed, and I was looking at the scene from much farther away. In the panoramic vista before me, I could see that the lamb was headed toward a cliff. The shepherd could see the cliff due to his height, but the lamb was completely unaware of the danger. As it turned out, the shepherd was tapping on the lamb out of love, redirecting its steps toward a safe path.

As I sought the Lord for understanding, I realized I was the little lamb. "Perhaps," I thought out loud, "what I consider as discomfort and pain is actually God's redirection. Maybe it's not always about being comfortable; maybe it's about trusting God and the path He is laying out before me."

The more I prayed, the more I felt led to follow up with Bob's company and find out more about their position. After much prayer, both alone and with friends from my church home group, as well as discussions with my children and family and after three separate interviews with the company, I accepted their generous offer.

Now came the difficult part: notifying those in charge at my current job. As I walked into the acting manager's office to inform her that I'd accepted another position, she said she had news for me. Upper management found out there were three employees on my team who'd been in cahoots with one another and had called into the company's hotline number anonymously, leaving incriminating comments in a voice message regarding other employees. Their comments spurred an internal investigation, and it was discovered their reports had been fabricated.

As it turned out, the employees' actions had been motivated by fear, and their calls and comments were an attempt to sabotage others in order to secure their own positions. Their actions were the very cause of their own demise.

My heart ached for the individuals involved in this scheme and the consequences they would inevitably have to endure due to their choices. I prayed for each one of them individually and asked God for his mercy upon them. "Oh Lord, I pray that they would know you, that they would find help and hope in you, and that most of all, they would learn to trust in you."

My assignment of providing a list of names was no longer necessary, as I would be the fourth person leaving the department. On my last day of work, I had only two things to remove from my desk to take with me: a picture of the children and me with Riviera—I looked at the picture every day as I struggled through various situations, because I never wanted to forget why I was there or why I could never give in or give up—and a greeting card that I'd had matted and framed. I looked at the card daily, prompted by a need to stay safely distanced from any painful choices made by others who had crossed my path. On the card were these few simple words by Horace Greeley:

Fame is vapor, popularity an accident, and riches take wings.
Only one thing endures, and that is character.

As I climbed into my car and drove away from my workplace for the very last time, a calmness came over me, as well as a peace I had never quite felt the entire time while working there. I had always felt unsettled but never knew exactly why. Now, I was heading in another direction, uncertain of what lay ahead, yet feeling very confident that everything happening was part of God's will and plan for me and my life.

As I drove down the road I played one particular song over and over again: "You Are in Control" by Scott Underwood. The song was on a CD that had been a gift to me as a first-time guest to the church I now considered my own house of worship. The lyrics encouraged a walk of faith built on trust, which was just what I needed as I ventured out once again, relying on my loving God to be the one in control, the one to direct my path.

The following Monday morning, as I prepared to start my third job in less than a year, I thought, *This is something I never would have dreamed I'd be doing.* As someone who preferred staying in one place, this third job change in so short a time was very uncomfortable for me. Nevertheless, there I was, driving to work.

As I entered the new office with muffins in hand, the staff greeted me with welcoming smiles and kind words. It didn't take long for my nervousness to settle down and my knees to stop knocking. My work experience would be helpful here, but I was most excited that I was right where God had placed me. This filled my heart with thanksgiving, and now, more than anything else, I wanted to honor my God by doing the very best job I could do for my new employer.

After evaluating the needs of the company and the department I would be overseeing, I obtained approval to hire one more person to join my team. I quickly picked up the telephone and called Sarah, the woman I had supervised in my first position, whose paychecks had been altered. She had been searching for a new job and quickly accepted my offer to come on board.

I was amazed by the full circle that took place, including the relationships in both my prior positions. I was able to share the good news of a loving God in my most recent past position. At that same company, I also made a new friend who would later inspire the children and me to get bicycles and ride for miles. That in itself was a blessing for us as we dealt with the emotional ups and downs during the ongoing criminal cases and the stress of trying to fit into a world which felt foreign to us. It was an especially healthy outlet for Christopher. And right smack in the center of it all was an intense crash course on how to walk by faith.

Not a day went by that didn't find me on my knees giving thanks or holding on to God's Word and his promises to help us get through another challenge. I was given constant opportunities to rely on and trust in God each day of my life, and oh, how I desperately wanted to know God more. It was God's wisdom and love, his covering and provision, his acceptance and direction, and his will that I constantly craved and sought, for under God's wings I felt safe. And truthfully, it was in those times when I felt the most helpless that I grew the most. In hindsight, I see that everything I went through helped to build a more intimate and permanent relationship with God, one based on total faith and trust. This was the relationship for which I had longed all of my life, but I had never been able to find it in another human being. This one was totally unconditional, complete, and without reservation.

Now, I was working with two people from my first place of employment, and I never would have known about this new position if not for meeting Bob at my first job. In fact, this position didn't even exist when I moved to town. Over time, it became more apparent just how blessed we were, not only with employment but with the ability to work for such an honorable company and a entrepreneur who ran his business from a position of strength and integrity.

"Trust in the Lord with all your heart, and lean not on your own understanding; In all your ways acknowledge Him, and He shall direct your paths" *(Proverbs 3:5-6 NKJV).*

Chapter 16

Holding On

Within the first year at my new job, the department's measurable success rate exceeded expectations, and things were looking great. But the children and I faced personal changes, which many times felt like more than we could handle. Calls from the district attorney's office became more frequent, and subpoenas arrived. The dreadful nightmare of our past was beginning to resurface. What little reprieve we'd experienced in getting our lives back together ended abruptly.

"You and Emily will receive a subpoena in the mail, Wendy," the district attorney explained. "We need both of you up here for the trial. I expect it to last for at least a week, and I may need you here for the entire time, so you will need to plan for accommodations."

It had been approximately fifteen months since the men were arrested. Neither criminal case had gone to final sentencing yet. Months of plea bargaining had transpired. The two men's cases were tried separately, and I was told that each one was trying to testify against the other in hope of reducing his own sentence.

Then an official notice from the court system arrived in the mail. My arms went weak, my head went light, and I began to shake as I folded the perforations back and forth in order to open it. Breaking the news to my daughter felt like a dagger going through my heart. I cried inside when I saw the look on her face.

I immediately notified the counselor at her school of what was to come. The counselor had been very supportive of my children and especially my daughter. There were many days when Emily would show up in her office because something in class had caused her to flee. A comment or an action would ignite her pain once again, leaving her with the sensation of not fitting in and not wanting to be there. I was so very grateful for my sister-in-law, who faithfully picked up Emily early from school on each of those days while I was at work.

"Wendy, the previously scheduled court date has been canceled. You can disregard the date noted on the subpoena," the district attorney informed me over the phone. "I will call you when it is rescheduled." Relief came but only for a moment, as I received another phone call from the district attorney shortly thereafter. "I'll let you know when to come up. I know it's a long drive, so I suggest you have your things packed because once I call, you'll need to be here by the following morning."

Oh no! I thought. *I have to inform my new boss about the subpoena. I don't want to tell him, but I don't want to lose my job either! Oh, what am I going to do?*

With all the courage I could muster, backed by a nightlong procession of prayers, I showed the owner of the company the subpoena and quietly explained the dilemma I was facing. His words were kind and compassionate as he shared his regrets and assured me I would still have a job when I returned. *Wow, I never could have done that at my last job,* I thought as I thanked God for this new job with such an understanding owner.

The district attorney had informed me the night before that she would call in the morning, but by one o'clock in the afternoon, I still had not heard from her. My palms and forehead were covered with sweat; my anxiety kept building as I waited for the telephone to ring. As I sat at my desk, I told myself, "Wendy, you can't just sit here waiting. You need to keep busy." I grabbed some papers off my desk that required photocopying and headed over to the copier.

As I stood there ready to make copies, thoughts of facing the man who had betrayed my trust and injured my child all those years plagued my mind. "I don't want to face him!" I cried under my breath. Then, as I reached to open the copier lid, all I could see were white blotches.

"Wendy, are you okay?" one of the employees asked as she walked up to me. She was just in time to catch me as my body went limp, my eyes rolled back, and I fainted over the copier.

Staff members helped to lay my body gently on the floor, and the owner was quickly summoned. He had a clear understanding of what might have caused me to faint, so he called Brad and Amy, who were listed as my emergency contacts. Each was only minutes away and came running to my aid.

The call from the district attorney never came that day, and eventually we were informed that a plea bargain had been reached. *It must be God's mercy and grace*, I thought, *that has spared Emily and me from having to sit through a face-to-face trial and sentencing with that man.* So one trial was down, but I knew we still had one more to go. Over the next few months we received phone calls from the district attorney's office, informing us of the progression of the second criminal case and the plea-bargaining efforts they were continuing to seek.

The delays were wearing me down. I asked for prayer each week when at church and in my home group, as well as when I visited Amy on my lunch hour. I was trying to keep up with a new job and its duties as well as care for my children and their needs. And now my children and I were juggling the never-ending emotional nightmare of an ongoing trial that constantly reminded us of the terror we had been though in our painful past. I felt like I was being swallowed up inside. *It's time for a deeper face-to-face with God*, I thought as I set everything else aside and snuggled up in my chair with a hot cup of coffee in one hand and my Bible in the other.

As I called out to God for his mercy and help, I saw a picture in my mind of a turbulent and stormy ocean, and there I was, right in the middle of it. I was trying desperately to keep my head above water, but I was starting to go under. Then, I felt the Lord's spirit speak to me in this picture, saying, "Wendy, all you have to do is hold on." The picture changed and instead of my being buried under the water, I was suddenly lying across the top of a big, flat, round yellow raft with handles around its side. The stormy seas were tossing me from side to side with each new swell. The crashing waters were smashing down upon me, but as long as I held on, I stayed afloat, no matter how furious the storm or raging seas became.

As I pondered this vision, it was clear to me that the yellow raft represented the Lord, my Savior and refuge in times of trouble. I needed to hold on to the Lord, along with his promises, and trust in his faithfulness and love, rather than focusing on the circumstances surrounding me. I was quickly reminded of and turned to the Scripture in Philippians 4:6 (NIV), which says, "Do not be anxious about anything, but in every situation, by prayer and petition, with thanksgiving, present your requests to God."

For the next six months, each month was filled with subpoenas which were subsequently canceled and rescheduled for the following month. I found myself easily overwhelmed in this never-ending interaction with the district attorney. Only this time, I remembered the image of the yellow raft that God had so graciously given me. I say "graciously" because I still was having a difficult time remembering things, and the visions God gave me were just what I needed to help me remember the things he was telling me. *Wendy, all you have to do is hold on,* I reminded myself. *Hold on to the Lord, and don't let go; just keep holding on, and he'll hold you up.*

I remembered God's promise in Isaiah 43:2 (NLT) that says, "When you go through deep waters, I will be with you. When you go through rivers of difficulty, you will not drown."

It had been over two years since the men were first arrested, and finally, the second trial date arrived. I sat close to Emily's side in the courtroom, with family and friends surrounding us with love and support. When it was my turn to speak, I began shaking as I nervously stood up on behalf of my daughter. With a quiver in my voice and tears welling up in my eyes, I looked directly at the judge and pleaded, "Your Honor, Branton could have been the hero in this story. He could have been the one to stop the nightmare and save my daughter from further abuse when he was invited into this horrific act, but instead, he chose to join in. And for this, Your Honor, he deserves the same severity of sentence as the other man involved."

"Your comment made him nervous," the district attorney whispered to me as the defense attorney quickly jumped to his feet and pointed in my direction in a cunning attempt to divert the blame from his client's actions. "If anyone should have known and stopped it," the defense attorney bellowed, "it should have been the mother!"

As much as I recognized his words as a manipulative ploy, a sudden tidal wave of guilt came crashing down upon me like nothing I'd ever felt before. *I didn't know*, I silently cried. *I didn't know ...*

Emily's head turned quickly in my direction, and I could see the concern in her eyes. *But why didn't I know?* I asked myself. *I should have known, just like he said. I should have known and saved her.* Tears ran uncontrollably down my face as the roaring waves of guilt pounced upon my conscience, stopping even my breath for a moment.

I had been dealing with grief and regret for months. I had been through numerous counseling sessions, trying to understand how it could have happened. I was trying to grasp how a predator's mind and actions worked so as to never allow such a person like that into our lives again. I experienced the pain of loss, great remorse, and overwhelming sorrow and shame for making a choice that allowed someone into our lives who would end up hurting my child. But through all of that, never had I looked at it as guilt.

Now, with the attorney's words flashing through my mind over and over again, I felt a helplessness and tormenting guilt backed by questions like, *Why didn't I make different choices? Why did I ever let anyone into my life after Mitch left us in the first place?* The waves of guilt were swallowing me up inside. All I could do now was hold on to the big yellow raft that was my Lord and Savior, Jesus Christ, the one who died on the cross and forgave me of all my sins before I ever even committed them. *I made the mistake of putting all my faith and trust in a human*, I told myself, *but now I can see that the only safe place to put my faith and trust is in the loving arms of my God, the author of mercy and grace.*

I agonized as I tried to remember if there were signs that I'd missed. What should I have seen or done? Thinking back to the couple of months right before the arrest, I could recall feeling something was wrong, but I couldn't put my finger on it. Even though I experienced those feelings, I never once suspected it was associated with Emily. I only remember that the man I married was not acting like himself—and as I fought to think back, a haunting remembrance came to mind.

Lawrence and I had just returned from having dinner with friends. When we got home, Emily was crying profusely. I ran to her, trying desperately to figure out what was wrong. As it turned out, Emily had taken pills with alcohol, and the alcohol caused her to throw up the pills. It appeared as though she had attempted to take her own life.

"But why? Why?" I asked her. Emily wouldn't answer me and instead only cried. I helplessly held her in my arms and then set up an emergency counseling appointment for her. I anxiously sat in the waiting room, with Lawrence by my side. I fervently hoped the counselor could help her.

Eventually, the counselor called both Lawrence and me into the room where she and Emily sat, only to inform us that Emily's actions had been brought on by Lawrence's abusively cussing at her when I was not around. I could only recall one incident—I'd arrived home from work, and I raced into Emily's room because I'd heard her crying. I found her pinned up against the wall by Lawrence, who was angrily yelling at her. When I asked him what was going on, he said he was tired of her rebellious attitude and attributed his actions, which he insisted were justifiable, to her "defiant and unruly age," as he put it. His anger frightened me, and I told him he was never allowed to put his hand on her again. I told him I would be the one to discipline her if she needed it.

The counselor had warned Lawrence in that session, "As someone working in law enforcement, you see a lot of ugly stuff, but your stepdaughter is not that stuff!" Then she insisted, "I need a formal commitment from you that you will not use profanity around Emily any longer and that you will treat her with dignity and respect"; he agreed.

It was during that appointment that Emily asked to live with her father, but I said that was not an option. Mitch was unemployed and basically destitute, living in between his parents' home and his friends' homes. *Oh, why didn't I see it? Why didn't I get it?* I screamed inside as I looked back.

They say hindsight is twenty-twenty. Knowing what I know now, I could see that Emily was being threatened all along in order to keep her quiet—so much so that when she had the chance to tell, all she could say was that Lawrence was yelling and cussing at her. He had her so convinced that I would end my life if I ever found out the truth that she may have thought her only way out was to end her own life.

Why didn't I get it? Emily was an outgoing, A+ student who was on the Principal's List, aspired to be a physician, and never missed a day of school in over three years. But then she became more reclusive, spending most of her time sitting alone in her room, reading. Her only outside interest seemed to be teaching sign language to the elementary students on her free period at school. Not only was she interested in learning sign language but also in teaching others an expression designed to help those without a voice of their own.

As I poured my heart out to God, weeping and sobbing over the choices I had made that ignorantly took the children and me down the painful path, God spoke to my heart. If I had known the truth about the man I married, I never would have married him. If I had known my daughter was being abused,

I would have done everything in my power to stop it, even to the point of my own death. My head understood these things, but my heart and soul were buried in guilt and regret, and I didn't know what to do about it. So I prayed, "Lord, how do I get past this guilt? I cannot change the past, and it's crippling me and ripping me up inside. Will it ever get better? Will Emily and Christopher ever truly forgive me?" This question led me down a very wide road called forgiveness, because now, not only did I need to forgive others, but I had to learn how to forgive myself as well.

I first began to grasp the truth about forgiveness with my own mother after the arrest. It was through my personal experience of God's loving me and answering my cry for help when I didn't do anything to deserve it that also taught me how to make allowances and forgive others for what I saw as their imperfections.

Through God's love and understanding, I learned there was a difference between the act that was done, the person who did it, and the healthy choices and boundaries on my part that could follow. I realized that by forgiving someone, I was not actually proclaiming what that person did was okay, or that it should be pushed aside or forgotten. In the case of my child and the abuse that she went through, it was not okay, and it will never be okay, not now or in the future. Our legal system has set up consequences for such actions.

I noticed how horrible unforgiveness felt, and like bondage, it was holding me in my pain. It was robbing me of any peace or rest within and blocking me from a deeper walk with God. I once heard the director of my women's Bible study say that holding a grudge or being resentful is like drinking an entire bottle of poison and hoping the other person will die from it. Pastor and author Ed Piorek explains forgiveness best in *The*

Father Loves You—An Invitation to Perfect Love when he describes it as ripping up the "I owe you."

It's true, I thought. I could be holding on to unforgiveness my entire life, thinking that the one who wronged me owes me for his terrible deed. But what if I never saw that person again, and he lived his life without any clue of the pain he caused me? And what if he passed away? Who was actually suffering? I was!

The more I thought about it, the more it made sense to close my eyes and go directly to my Lord in prayer over every person who offended or hurt me and visually see myself tearing up the "I owe you" that I was harboring in my heart toward each of them. As I closed my eyes, I also pictured myself surrendering the anger, disappointment, disapproval, frustration, judgment, depression, regret, sorrow, fear, and hurt, to name just a handful—they were like weeds being plucked from the soil of my heart. I pictured myself laying them down at the feet of Jesus and letting the Lord lovingly take them away from me and replace them with new seeds of love, mercy, grace, kindness, compassion, wisdom, and understanding.

Through studying Dr. Henry Cloud and Dr. John Townsend's books *Boundaries* and *Changes That Heal*, I was able to build up confidence and set healthy boundaries in my own life as well. I wanted a healthy and safe environment for myself and my children. I heard Pastor Rick Warren mention in his messages that "Hurt people will hurt people," and we have a choice "to be bitter or better." *But how will I know if they are hurt or bitter? I wondered. Ultimately, how will I know if I will be safe?* Then I read Matthew 7:20—"by their fruits you will know them" (NKJV)—and I began to understand that whatever is on the inside will eventually show up on the outside, if not in public then surely in private. Understanding this made it even more important to stay close to the Lord, to continue to ask for his guidance, and to continue to listen.

Learning to forgive others was difficult, but it was easier than forgiving myself. When it came to self-forgiveness, I needed a lot more personal help. So down on my knees I went, crying out to my God for understanding. "Where do I start?" I asked the Lord in prayer.

These words came back in answer to me: *"Wendy, think of someone you love—someone who, no matter what he or she does wrong, you will still love."* I thought about my children. I thought about the times when they were disobedient or didn't listen. No matter how upset I got at them, I could never stop loving them. *"Well, Wendy,"* I heard a voice in my head respond, *"that's just a tiny little taste of the love I have for you. There isn't anything you can do that will ever stop me from loving you."*

Once again, the Lord answered my cry for help and showed me the first step in self-forgiveness was realizing that no matter what I did or how badly I messed up, I was loved—and not only was I loved, but I also was forgiven. God already knew I was not perfect, and because he gave me free will, he knew I would make choices, and in those choices I would make mistakes. This is exactly why Christ sacrificed himself on the cross for me. This is why he forgave me before I was even born—because God is love and because there isn't anything I could do that would ever separate his love from me. Gratefully, God's love will always remain the same.

Over and over again, I had to remind myself that I was loved and that I was forgiven. In that love, I found the courage to go to some of those people I hurt by my actions or by my choices and ask for forgiveness, beginning with my children. The deeper I felt God's love and forgiveness in my own heart, the more I felt set free. I was so very grateful to the Lord for his mercy and grace that all I wanted to do was to love God right back.

I experienced what John talks about: "We love because he first loved us" (1 John 4:19 NIV). God taught me how to love by loving me first. When I searched the Word of God to better understand how to love God in return, I found John 14:15, which says, "If you love me, obey my commandments" (NLT). These words gave me an even deeper desire to follow God's Word, his will, and his direction. No matter what, I knew I never wanted to breathe another breath of life without my God being front and center.

The more time I spent with God, the more verses he gave me along the way to encourage and provide hope—verses that told me he was with me and that I was accepted, chosen, wanted, loved, and adored; verses which told me I was my Lord's beloved. I became aware that my identity was no longer determined by the things I had done or by other peoples' opinions of me but by the one who died on the cross for me. I began to understand that I am the Lord's little lamb. I am a child of God. I am a daughter of the King.

"What a person desires is unfailing love."
—Proverbs 19:22 (NIV)

Chapter 17

The Power of a Promise

God knew exactly what he was doing when he placed me in my new job. I was blessed both with the excitement of a new challenge and with the appreciation I received for a job well done. I was close to home and able to maneuver through the subpoenas and hearings. Being close to our home, the school, and our counselor's office also made our numerous visits possible during my lunch hour. Yes, once again I could see that every little detail had been tended to by God and to aid in my children's and my pathway toward healing.

As I drove to work one morning, I was overcome with gratitude for all the miracles and blessings from God, and I began talking to him. "Lord," I said with a smile on my face, "from the very beginning, we were helped by family and friends and given a place to sleep when we no longer had a home. And Lord, we were helped financially and even chosen by the Victim Witness Program to receive their gifts as family of the year. Wow, Lord, I am overcome with appreciation as I think about how we were blessed in so many ways by so many people."

My heart was so filled with thanksgiving that I ended my conversation with a request. "Lord, the tithing I give you is not enough. I want to be able to help others too, the same way I've been helped. Would you please help me to be able to do that, Lord? Would you please help me grow financially so I not only can take care of my children but also be used by you to help others in the same way they have helped me?" By the time I arrived at work, a peace and comfort had settled within my soul, and somehow I knew that God had heard my request and understood my longing.

Within the first three months of my employment, my immediate supervisor left the company, and I was given an increase in pay. Then, over time, the company's sales grew and a need for more oversight increased, prompting the owner to hire a consultant. My department had made tremendous strides, and our accounts were doing very well. Because of this, the owner asked the consultant to focus on the other departments that required her assistance. Eventually, when the consultant's contract was ending, she expressed an interest in being hired on full time.

Even though the owner had asked the consultant to focus on other departments, she began to pressure my staff and me with questions and condescending remarks. The owner asked her to stop, but she didn't let up; she only did it more discreetly. She would come to my desk after everyone else in the office had gone home, telling me I wasn't doing enough to bring the accounts receivable current, despite the considerable strides we were making each month. The owner was happy with the work my team had accomplished, and I had trouble understanding the consultant's motivation. I thought, *Perhaps her actions are coming from a need to convince others that we cannot survive without her.*

Nevertheless, her comments and actions became more difficult each day. Her behavior escalated over several months, and my sensitivity to such conduct made it even more difficult for me personally. Then one morning, she directed another outburst of disrespectful words toward me in front of my staff. Their faces showed surprise at the consultant's aggressive words, and I felt tears welling up inside. I turned my head quickly so my subordinates couldn't see me, and I drove home for lunch that day with tears pouring from my eyes. I could think only about running toward a safe haven, a place where I could spend time with the Lord. I needed his strength and his comforting reprieve. As I walked into the house, I looked around at all the blessings the children and I had received from God. The old Wendy would have completely broken down and run away in her pain, looking for an escape, but the new Wendy was running to the Lord with her pain.

As tears continued to stream down my cheeks, I looked up toward the ceiling and said, "Dear Lord, I know you gave this wonderful home to the children and me, and I appreciate it so much, but I am afraid I cannot stay. I don't think I can last any longer at my job." Just as quickly as I cried out, I heard the Lord speak to me, the words bellowing clearly through my mind: *"I want you there. I'll work it out."*

Receiving this personal promise from the Lord instilled in me a newfound hope and confident assurance. I knew that as I continued to choose to trust God and ask him to be the one in control of my life, like a loving father he would be there to watch over and protect me. The words that God spoke to me also confirmed I was right where God wanted me to work and right where he had chosen for the children and me to rest our heads and sleep at night. I was filled with gratitude to my Lord and Savior for his love and protection, as well as the direction he continued to provide.

As I entered the office after lunch that day, I felt like a new person. I walked with confidence and found it easy to remain professional and courteous when confronted with opposition. I was right where God said he wanted me to be, and from that day forward, I chose to remain secure in that word from my Lord. And in doing so, I also found the freedom to stay focused on the company's success and what I was hired to do, rather than on another person's opinion or bitterness toward me. *It's God's opinion that matters most*, I thought. As long as I knew I was right where he wanted me to be, I was grounded and could continue to stand strong.

Soon afterward, I was reading about the life of Joseph and the coat of many colors in the book of Genesis. I experienced an "aha" moment as I felt another burst of hope unleash. I read how Joseph was mistreated and went through years of difficulty, yet in it, he had the Lord's favor over him. Ultimately, all he had to hold onto was a dream, a promise from God that let him know things would turn around and be better in the end. Joseph held on to that promise and never turned his back on God from the very first day he was sold into slavery, locked away in prison, and ultimately chosen by Pharaoh and put in charge of all Egypt. Eventually, God's promise was fulfilled, and rather than vengeance, Joseph's heart, which was saturated in God's love and filled with God's wisdom, showed mercy on his family, saving them from famine and reuniting all of them once again.

In the months to follow, as I maneuvered through each workday, I held on to the promise God had given me: *"I want you there. I'll work it out."* The consultant's temporary contract was extended, and the best way for me to face each new day was to first spend time with the Lord in prayer each morning. I would pray and then quietly listen, after filling my heart and mind with the many promises in his Word. I grew in strength and inner peace as I read God's Word:

"You can sleep without fear; you need not be afraid of disaster or the plots of wicked men, for the Lord is with you; he protects you" (Proverbs 3:24 LB).

"He will cover you with his feathers, and under his wings you will find refuge; his faithfulness will be your shield and rampart. You will not fear the terror of night, nor the arrow that flies by day" (Psalm 91:4-5 NIV).

"Let all who take refuge in you be glad ... you surround them with your favor as with a shield" (Psalm 5:11-12 NIV).

"The Lord is the stronghold of my life—of whom shall I be afraid?" (Psalm 27:1 NIV).

"I keep my eyes always on the Lord. With him at my right hand, I will not be shaken" (Psalm 16:8 NIV).

As flashes of the Sermon on the Mount came to mind, I found my heart changing, and I wanted to pray for others rather than hold a grudge, most especially against the consultant. I pulled out my Bible and turned to Matthew 5:44. "Love your enemies, bless those who curse you, do good to those who hate you, and pray for those who spitefully use you" (NKJV).

Oh, how I love the advice and wisdom I find in the Bible, I thought. It helps me walk out my life in a much healthier and peaceful way.

The more I prayed for those who had wounded me and those for whom I would have harbored bitterness in the past, the more I experienced a sense of peace; I felt a new compassion toward them instead. I could see a difference taking place within me. In the past, I would have felt frustrated and out of control. I would have ended up depressed and angry at the world, yet hiding it all inside as I turned that anger inward, hurting nobody more deeply than myself. Now, as I experienced God's love filling me up, I saw that it couldn't help but spill out toward others in my path. Instead of feeling empty, I felt empathy.

Eight months later, the consultant was no longer with the company, and I was eventually offered a promotion with additional responsibilities. My perseverance and trusting in God and his promise to me had been rewarded. New challenges continued to arise, but I was practicing going to God first. There were days when I closed my office door just to bend a knee at my chair. I continually went to God for help and advice as I maneuvered through the obstacles of each new day.

Before I knew it, the five-year anniversary date of the end of my daughter's nightmare arrived. I was at work and heading out the front door for lunch when all of the sudden it hit me. If I had known five years earlier what I knew now—that I would be vice president of business operations for an upstanding company, that the children's and my needs would be met, and that I would be able to financially help out others as we had been helped—I would not have spent so much time in fear, doubt, and worry. I would not have fallen apart with so much anxiety. I would have spent more time laughing and being filled with anticipation and excitement, always eager to see what God was going to do in our lives next. *Knowing this now*, I thought, *truly helps me look at my life, today and tomorrow, differently.*

Through this realization, I faced difficult situations in a new way. It was easier to face them head on and with hope, proclaiming the promise of Proverbs 2:7–8. "He holds success in store for the upright ... he guards the course of the just and protects the way of his faithful ones" (NKJV). I began to say thank you to God, even when I could not see the light at the end of the tunnel, as I stood in the promise of Jeremiah 29:11. "'For I know the plans I have for you,' declares the Lord, 'plans to prosper you and not to harm you, plans to give you hope and a future'" (NIV). I could trust in and rely on my Lord to be with me and never to leave me, never to turn his back on me, and never to let go of me. He was a God who would not only help me through life's challenges but also take whatever seemed to be going wrong and turn it for good and for his purpose and pleasure.

It was like the song of freedom and independence that came as an answer to me in the shower that morning, when I asked if I should stay in the house or sell. Or the promise I saw in God's Word, telling me he had prepared a place for us when we were unexpectedly homeless. And then there was the "I want you there. I'll work it out" message when I didn't think I could last another day at my job. In each case, as with many other encounters with God, a hope grew. These promises were not only something to hold on to, but they changed the way I handled new situations. I found inner courage and confidence to navigate the challenges in front of me. God gave me promises that were meant to encourage and keep me from being pulled down into a pit of despair and anxiety. God gave me a reason to not give up, and God taught me how to trust him more—something I learned would take a constant and daily choice.

My birthday arrived and my sister-in-law gave me a book titled *Avoiding Mr. Wrong* by Stephen Arterburn and Dr. Meg

J. Rinck. God had not been the center of either of my prior marriages, and that was something I longed for, so Amy's giving me this book made total sense. I had been talking about wanting to have a wholesome relationship someday— someday, when the children were older, and I felt emotionally and spiritually healthy myself. I thanked her for the book, knowing it was given in love, but as soon as I was alone, I burst into tears.

It was Saturday night, and as I filled up my oval bathtub, I cried, "I know I don't trust in my own ability to choose the right man, but this book only confirms the fact that nobody else trusts in my ability either!" I couldn't stop sobbing and began to wonder what filled my bathtub more—water from the faucet or my tears. "God, could I really end up with another man like the last one?" I wailed. "Could I end up marrying another predator? How will I know? What if I can't tell? I couldn't tell before, so could this really happen to me again? Lord, that was before I really knew you! That was before I recognized the promptings of your Holy Spirit inside me. You wouldn't let that happen to me again, would you, Lord?" I was filled with both sorrow and panic at the possibility.

I went to bed that night with tears on my pillow and woke up later than usual the next morning with bloodshot eyes. When I arrived at church, the sanctuary was already filled to capacity, and I settled into one of the last seats in the very back row. I soon realized the reason for the larger attendance was that a special guest was visiting from out of town. His name was John Paul Jackson, an evangelist with a prophetic ministry, who shared a powerful message about our loving God and the gifts of the Holy Spirit.

At the end of the message, John Paul Jackson asked several people in the congregation to stand up, and he explained he felt led to share a word with them, which he did. They each seemed quite touched by what he said. Then, when it seemed as if the service was about to end, he paused for one more moment and pointed to the back of the sanctuary in my direction. He asked for the woman in the back with the brown hair to please stand. I looked around the area to see who he was talking about—and finally realized he was speaking to me. I pointed to myself, and he said, "Yes, you. Please stand up."

As I slowly stood, I could see friends from my home group just a few rows to my left; they were smiling at me. Then John Paul Jackson said, "Miss, I feel the Lord wants you to know that sorrow is at night, but joy comes in the morning, and this will never happen to you a second time. Your heart will be healed, and you will learn to trust again."

Tears flowed from my eyes as I listened to his words. God had spoken to me personally before, but this time, it was as if God wanted to make sure I really heard him, because he gave me a promise so loud that not only did I hear it, but so did every other person in the congregation. As the service ended, friends encouraged me with great big hugs. They were aware of my story and the need for healing. They also had prayed for my children and me on numerous occasions. But there wasn't anybody but God who knew about my painful night of weeping that transpired in my oval tub only hours before.

I thought about the miraculous words given to me in the service and the promise that my heart would be healed. *Could I really learn to trust again?* I wondered. The thought of my being able to do this seemed a million miles away, yet at the same time, the promise of a better tomorrow brought joy and hope back into my heart. "That was God loving me! It was a manifestation of his loving kindness and his mercy and grace," I said to myself. "I wasn't just picked out of the crowd or given a word because I did something special to deserve it. As a matter of fact, I was even late to church. No, it was God's merciful love pouring down on me." As deep as God knew my pain, that was as loud as he spoke his promise over me, shattering the very fear of hopelessness that had gripped my heart just the night before.

Since the first day I cried out to God, he had been answering me. It took a while for me to realize this, but when I did, like the story of Peter in Matthew 14:22-33, when Christ called him out of the boat, so has my heart been for Jesus as I've jumped out of my own boat and run toward my Savior. And, just as in the case of Peter, I too begin to sink each moment I take my eyes off Jesus and allow the overwhelming storms of life and the circumstances surrounding me to catch me off guard and steal my focus, steal my hope, and try to steal my faith.

The only way I've been able to stay afloat, as in the vision of the yellow raft, is to keep my eyes on Jesus, focus on his words, and hold on to his promises. I have to wrap God's assurance around my waist like a life preserver and constantly choose to never let go, no matter the circumstances.

One of the best ways I found to hold on to God's promises is by recording them in a journal. I write down encouraging Scriptures, ones that speak life and hope to my heart. I also document impressions I feel God giving me during the day or at night and in my prayer time. My journal is also filled with letters to God. Sometimes I am crying out to him, and other times I am merely reflecting on my gratitude for him. But in either case, when I ponder long enough, I am always able to make a list of ways I saw his hand over my life, for which I offer him my thanks.

The more I asked God to take over the driver's seat of my life, the better able I was to handle the situations in my daily life. But I had one particular challenge where I needed God's constant help and guiding light—the continuous battle I had with fear. Fear could rise up out of nowhere. It could instantly be set off by the slightest stimulus. A comment, a memory, or even a smell could get the ball rolling. It would first attack my thoughts and then manifest itself through my emotions and paralyze me in my tracks.

I was amazed at how quickly I found myself turning my head toward the storm—how instantly I could plummet downward into a murky sea of anxiety, worry, and doubt. I wondered how I could fall so quickly after all God had done for me. God had never let me down since the day I cried out to him, yet I was still fighting this relentless battle with fear over my children and their welfare and over my circumstances and my choices. I had a fear of being hurt and of being incapable or not good enough. I struggled with the fear of letting someone down or making a mistake. I fought the fear of being unworthy, a failure, or misunderstood. Then there was the fear of someone's taking advantage of me, as well as the fear of not being accepted. I was plagued with the fear of disapproval and of not measuring up to the standards of those around me. Life had taught me I should always fear that I would be let down. And I can't leave out the debilitating fear of being judged and rejected by others, and over it all, the overwhelming fear of being left and being all alone.

In all my humanness, and however many times I'd hold on to a promise or turn to God for help and direction, I realized the Enemy was right there on the sidelines, toying with me like a cat does a mouse, trying to get my eyes off Jesus. The Enemy spoke words of doubt and reasons for worry, and he tried eagerly to kill, steal, and destroy all hope by putting my eyes on the storm, especially during those times when faith told me to hold on, but the evidence of God's intervention or answer could not be seen.

I read, "The thief does not come except to steal, and to kill, and to destroy. I have come that they may have life, and that they may have it more abundantly" (John 10:10 NKJV).

"So that's what is going on!" I exclaimed. It was apparent the first thing I needed to do was learn how to recognize these lies of the Enemy that would attack my mind and try to take me down. These fears were based on the old life of Wendy, the life where Jesus was not invited to be a part. Second, I needed to remember that Satan could not take away the truth or my faith unless I let him. This meant I needed to gear up. I needed powerful weapons to fight this battle, and that's exactly what I found when I read through the Bible. I found hundreds of promises, all filled with hope, all ready to attack any fear, doubt, and worry I might come across.

Also, John 10:10 told me that Jesus came to bring life, not take it away. And most comfortingly, in the same chapter, Jesus explained that his sheep know him and can hear his voice. "Yes, that's exactly what I need to fight this battle!" I exclaimed. "I need my shepherd! I need to hear what he has to say. I need his promises to sustain me. I need to replace those fears, doubts, and worries with the promises of God."

I needed to stay close to the shepherd and trust him, just as in the vision I had earlier of the little lamb that would have gone over the cliff without the shepherd directing its path. Then I read, "Give yourselves humbly to God. Resist the devil and he will flee from you. And when you draw close to God, God will draw close to you" (James 4:7–8 LB).

I began doing self-checks and practicing how to recognize the lies of the Enemy. "Okay, Wendy, did that thought cause you anxiety? How about depression? Anger or fear? How about worry or doubt? Helplessness or hopelessness? Did it start with 'I can't' or end with 'So what? Nobody cares'?" As thoughts came to mind, I would stop and ask myself these questions. Inevitably, I would hear that voice inside my head tell me something God would never say to my face, like "Wendy, you'll never be wanted, loved, or cared about ... you're not good enough." I was beginning to see the difference. I noticed if the thought was not backed by God's love—if it did not speak the truth about me or what is found in God's Word; if it did not edify and build up but instead tried to kill, steal, or destroy my life, my spirit, peace, or joy, then it most definitely was a lie. And that lie did not come from the person who made the comment but from the Enemy himself, in an attempt to defeat and deceive me by any means possible.

I studied what Jesus said when he was confronted by Satan and the lies of the Enemy. When Satan tempted Jesus after fasting forty days and forty nights, in Matthew 4, Jesus humbly yet powerfully refused to acknowledge what was being thrown at him and replied with truth and the Word of God. "Get out of here, Satan ..." (Matthew 4:10 NLT). And Jesus even rebuked Satan through Peter when he said, "Get behind me, Satan! You are a stumbling block to me" (Matthew 16:23 NIV).

I decided what I needed to do was to say the same things Jesus said. "That's it!" I told myself. "Each time my thoughts give way to fear or worry, and every time I find myself accepting the words or labels thrown on me by others—ones which do not speak the truth of who I am to God—I am going to speak out to that thought. I am going to use the very same words Jesus said, and I am going to replace those lies with the truth."

I found many more opportunities to practice this new plan than I want to admit. As thoughts flew toward me like fiery arrows, I would confront those thoughts with, "Get behind me, Satan! You cannot have your way with me! I belong to the Lord! I am his chosen one. I am a daughter of the King." I was astonished at how empowered I felt inside. Instead of the helpless agony I had experienced in the past, I felt like shaking the dust off my hands and walking away with a strut.

Next, I began listening to the words that came out of my own mouth. Did I speak life or death? Did I condemn or build up when I spoke to myself and others? "The tongue has the power of life and death" (Proverbs 18:21 NIV). I began examining myself, and I'm not proud about what I discovered. I repented and asked God to help me speak his truth and his love, rather than my own opinion or judgment. I needed to be filled up with God's love and compassion before it could start spilling out naturally. "For the mouth speaks what the heart is full of" (Luke 6:45 NIV).

Slowly, I saw a transformation take place that started in my heart and migrated to my head and out through my mouth. I would ask myself over and over again, *What would Jesus say to me or to the other person in this situation?* I could be sure that if it didn't glorify God, then it was not of him. I was learning to speak life and encouragement, rather than using words that went straight for the heart, destroying its target in an instant like a heat-seeking missile.

While visiting a family member's church, I heard Pastor Richard West speak on "Praying the Promise, Not the Problem." He shared, "We have the authority as believers, given to us in Christ Jesus, to bring heaven into earth." This concept of "praying the promise and not the problem" made total sense. Rather than focusing on the lies of the Enemy that come to kill, steal, and destroy my hope, faith, and peace—which caused me to focus on all that I *didn't* want instead of what I *did* want—why not focus on the truth and the power and claim the victory? After all, it falls in line with thanking God for the answers to my prayers. He's always answered. I just didn't always see the results right away. I've had to learn to stand in faith, knowing God hears and is working it out for my good.

As I thought about this concept, I saw an amazing correlation between my prayers and God's actions. When I first cried out to God, it was for help, and God helped me. I didn't cry, "Everything is horrible!" I already knew that, and God already knew that. I cried out for what I wanted. I wanted *help*. Later, I read, "Ask and it will be given you ... For everyone who asks receives" (Matthew 7:7–8 NIV). *Wait a minute*, I thought. *What is it I am asking for?*

"Say what you want, not what you don't want"—this was a communication technique I heard from Marshall Rosenberg and something I was teaching the staff at work. It was a comparable concept to praying the promise rather than the problem, so I sunk my teeth into it.

Some employees would come into my office and complain without end. They talked about what was wrong, who was wrong, and why everything was wrong. But I had a very difficult time getting them to tell me how they wanted it to be. "What would make it better?" I'd ask. "What kind of outcome would you like to see?" Some employees struggled terribly with focusing on a fix or a better outcome. "We need to have a destination in mind," I'd tell them, "before we can map out a way to get there." This was something I learned while reading Stephen R. Covey's book, *The 7 Habits of Highly Effective People*. It was Habit 2, "Begin with the End in Mind."

In the same way, claiming God's promises and praying his divine will and Word over the situation was something I wanted to start doing—not only over my own situations but over those I loved and cared about too. It wasn't just talking about the problem, I realized; it was talking to the problem and telling it where to go!

A great example of this is found in a story in Matthew. A furious storm hit the disciples by surprise while on their boat. The disciples panicked (I can relate to that) and ran to Jesus, who was still asleep on the boat. "Lord, save us! We are going to drown!" The words they cried out were definitely proclaiming doom and gloom. And what did Jesus do when he heard them say this? First, he questioned their faith. Then Jesus did exactly what he gave me the power to do through his Holy Spirit. "He got up and rebuked the winds and waves." And here's the happily-ever-after ending—everything became "completely calm" once again (Matthew 8:23–27 NIV).

I've heard a catchy little term of late, used mostly when one person thinks another needs to toughen up or deal with a difficult situation. Someone will say, "Well, I guess it's time to put on your big-boy pants." I laughed as I thought about it. "It's not my big-boy pants I need to put on; it's my 'promise pants'!" I exclaimed. I am much more capable, resourceful, and way more persevering when I step into the truth, which is that I am not alone, and I have a God who loves me and promises to help me along the way. I am much more successful when I hold on to the promises God has given me to live by than when I try to accomplish anything on my own.

My "promise pants" have God's promises written all over them. They tell me not to be afraid because my God is with me. "Do not be afraid, for I am with you" (Isaiah 43:5 NIV).

And he will never turn his back or abandon me. "Never will I leave you; never will I forsake you" (Hebrews 13:5 NIV).

The Lord's promises say that as I trust in him, he will direct my path. "Trust in the Lord with all your heart ... And He shall direct your paths" (Proverbs 3:5–6 NKJV).

And just like the story of how God helped the Israelites cross through the Red Sea when they were hemmed in (Exodus 14), my God makes a way for me where there seems to be no way. "You have freed me when I was hemmed in" (Psalm 4:1 AB).

The Lord is always willing to lend a hand. "For I am the Lord your God who takes hold of your right hand and says to you, Do not fear; I will help you" (Isaiah 41:13 NIV).

My God says to keep my eyes on him, and he will help me through anything I must face. "Just as you trusted Christ to save you, trust him, too, for each day's problems" (Colossians 2:6 LB).

And if I seek him first, everything else will fall into place. "Seek first his kingdom and his righteousness, and all these things will be given to you" (Matthew 6:33 NIV).

My promise pants are covered with words of wisdom and direction, lighting the path before me. "Your word is a lamp to my feet and a light to my path" (Psalm 119:105 AB).

My loving God leads the way, instilling courage in me to keep moving forward. "Be strong and courageous! Do not be afraid and do not panic ... For the Lord your God will personally go ahead of you. He will neither fail you nor abandon you" (Deuteronomy 31:6 NLT).

My God promises the best possible outcome. "Those who listen to instruction will prosper; those who trust the Lord will be joyful" (Proverbs 16:20 NLT).

And when I put my trust in God, I experience peace. "You will keep in perfect peace all who trust in you, all whose thoughts are fixed on you!" (Isaiah 26:3 NLT).

My promise pants say that if I start to slip, my God will catch me. "I lift up my eyes to the mountains—where does my help come from? My help comes from the Lord, the Maker of heaven and earth. He will not let your foot slip—he who watches over you will not slumber ... nor sleep" (Psalm 121:1–4 NIV).

They assure me that my God is ever faithful. "For you, Lord, alone make me dwell in safety and confident trust" (Psalm 4:8 AB).

And he will never change on me. "Jesus Christ is the same yesterday and today and forever" (Hebrews 13:8 NIV).

My promise pants remind me to rely on the Lord, and he will be my strength. "I can do all things through Christ who strengthens me" (Philippians 4:13 NKJV).

And that in him, I am a conqueror. "He who is in you is greater than he who is in the world" (1 John 4:4 NKJV).

Even if I don't seem to have any strength of my own, I still have a partner who is bigger than any obstacle, and he is always there to help me. "It is God who arms me with strength, And makes my way perfect" (Psalm 18:32 NKJV).

Yes, my promise pants are wrapped all around me with a love that's never-ending. "Nothing in all creation will ever be able to separate us from the love of God that is revealed in Christ Jesus our Lord" (Romans 8:37–39 NLT).

They remind me that I have a protector. "But let all who take refuge in you be glad ... you surround them with your favor as with a shield" (Psalm 5:11–12 NIV).

And they tell me to walk in trust, for God is my hope. "All things are possible with God" (Mark 10:27 NIV).

Chapter 18

Always a Choice

The alarm clock sent a startling shockwave through my body as it went off at five o'clock in the morning, waking me from a deep and silent sleep. It was Saturday, usually my time of rest or an adventurous outing, including a potential game of Ultimate Frisbee after a long workweek, but not this morning.

I arrived at my office at six o'clock, parked my car, and jumped into a coworker's vehicle, joining a couple of other employees from the office to head to an all-day seminar, ninety minutes away.

For the past six weeks, my Saturday mornings had been anything but a time of pleasure or reprieve. I was one of three from my company assigned to study the newly mandated federal and state regulations soon to take effect in our industry. This meant meeting together each Saturday to study, take weekly exams, and obtain our certifications prior to writing the additional compliance policies and procedures, as well as customer notifications, which would soon be required.

This particular Saturday was more challenging than others. I found it impossible to escape the drafty cold air forced down upon me through the air vents in the hotel's massive conference room. It was causing the symptoms of my sinus infection to flare up even more rapidly than usual. I had been fighting sinus infections for the past five years. At first, I only experienced them through the winter months, but eventually they began hitting me throughout the entire year on a monthly basis. At first it would only last a week to ten days, but gradually, I experienced more days with them than without.

As we were dismissed from the conference, I went racing into the bathroom with another nosebleed, a side effect from the continuous use of my nasal spray. Unfortunately, the bathroom delay only made things worse, as it left my coworkers irritated. It had been a long day, and we still had a long drive ahead of us, and I was holding them up.

From the look on my coworker's face, I decided I'd better jump into the backseat instead of the front seat for the ride home. There was an uncomfortable silence in the air, and I turned my face toward the back window, hoping the driver wouldn't see the tears welling up in my eyes. The sun was setting as we drove home, making it easier for me to hide my emotions in a backseat of darkness. As I sat there looking out the window, I couldn't help but notice just how tired and rundown I felt. My face felt flushed, and chills ran up and down my body. *Oh, my goodness*, I thought as I touched my cheeks and forehead. *I have a fever. No wonder I feel so terrible.*

As I continued to gaze out the window, noticing the various lights as we drove down the freeway, I began to have a very serious conversation with God. *You know what, God? I have been praying and asking you for healing for these sinus infections for a long time now, and you don't even seem to be listening. It's like you don't even care! I am so mad at you for not caring! I am so mad at you for allowing me to suffer like this, because I know you can heal me if you want to. I've seen what you can do. So why won't you heal me? You must not care about me anymore.*

Outward anger was an emotion I rarely felt, so I was chalking up this rage as a side effect of the fever, as if I needed to justify my thoughts to God and to myself. As soon as my coworker's car came to a complete stop in the parking lot next to my car, I hid my face and jumped out of his car, mumbling a quick thank-you and good-bye to avoid any further conversation. As I got in my car and glanced in the rearview mirror, I noticed black mascara lines running down my cheeks.

As I poured Epsom salts into my running bath that night, I thought, *This is a day I want to forget.* The oval tub, which I'd considered to be my "prayer closet," just turned into my crying chamber. A fever could very quickly make everything seem overwhelming, and the humiliation I had just gone through with my coworkers had pushed me over the edge. "I am supposed to be a leader," I cried, "but now they just see me as an annoyance!" Tears continued to pour down my face while bouts of self-pity and words of upset toward God spewed through my lips.

The following morning, as I slipped into a seat toward the back of the church, I was pleased the music was still playing, though I was surprised that I'd made it in time for the music after having to stand in a hot shower to relieve the throbbing pain in my sinuses. I arrived just in time to hear one more song that spoke words of love and God's tender mercy—everything I needed at that moment. As the last song ended, Pastor Mike asked if there was anyone who needed healing, and if so, to stand up right where he or she was. Then he asked for those around the ones standing to please pray for them as he also prayed for them from the pulpit.

Like a little girl running toward the open arms of her daddy, I leaped to my feet, forgetting for a moment just how furious I had been toward God only the night before. With my eyes closed and the palms of my hands laid out before me, as if ready to catch something falling toward me from heaven, I distantly heard Pastor Mike's voice say, "I am sensing the Lord wants to heal someone's sinuses today. If that's you, I want to encourage you to stand up and let us pray for you."

That's me, Lord! That's me! I cried from the very depths of my heart. Tears ran down my checks and over my lips as I silently mouthed the words once again, *That's me, Lord.* I felt the gentle touch of those around me placing their hands upon my shoulder and could faintly hear the loving and prayerful words spoken over me. There was an ever-so-slight blanket of warmth resting over the bridge of my nose as they prayed.

As I sat back down, gentleness rested upon me in church and stayed with me as the day progressed. I noticed the anticipated need to use my medicated nasal spray, which I used twice a day, never came. It was dinnertime, and I always required the use of the spray before I could eat, in order to breathe and chew at the same time. But I didn't seem to need it. The next morning, I woke up thinking I'd surely need to use my medication and nose spray, but it wasn't necessary. Day after day, week after week, the need to use the spray was never required again. I was instantly healed by the Lord during that moment of prayer in church and have never experienced another sinus infection since.

My heart was overflowing with thanksgiving and gratitude to my Lord Jesus Christ for rescuing me and healing my sinuses. And of course these prayers of thanksgiving were immediately followed by a very humbled spirit and many words of repentance and remorse for my attitude and the fact that I ever doubted my Savior's love or compassion for me in the first place.

I held off sharing the good news with the pastor until a month had passed, because I wanted to make sure the healing was genuine. The pastor was so excited when I told him the good news that he asked if I'd be willing to share what God had done with the entire congregation, which I happily agreed to do.

I shared with those in the sanctuary, saying, "If there was ever a time when I deserved to be healed the least, it was right when God healed me. I don't think I did anything to deserve it, and as a matter of fact, I am embarrassed to admit this, but I'd been angrily complaining to God just the night before that I didn't think he even cared about me anymore. And yet," I told the congregation, "in spite of my angry emotions, I still knew in my heart that God was still God. I suppose that might be why I was carrying on with him the way I was just the night before. My past experiences with the Lord had already proven to me that my Lord Jesus Christ had the ability to help and to heal me. I just had to continue to choose him instead of giving up or giving in. And just as the woman who reached out to grab the hem of Jesus's garment as he walked by and was instantly healed after twelve years, as told in Matthew 9:20–22, I too, in my own childlike way, immediately jumped to my feet, still running to my Lord for help when the opportunity for prayer was offered that day by the pastor. So many times I have found myself in a place, just like this one, where I know the only way out is through God." I then encouraged them to never give up on God, because after all, "We would never want God giving up on us."

I don't know why God chose to heal me right then and there, or why I struggled with the sinus infections for five years before being healed, yet in hindsight, the timing was absolutely perfect, as it truly confirmed it was not about my earning it but instead was based solely on the gracious love and generous mercy of God. I had sought help through normal medical means and had reached the point where all I had left was to seek my Lord. This was one more lesson, instilled in me once again, that the Lord does hear my prayers and is with me, no matter what the circumstances of the moment might be.

It was during the difficult days leading up to this healing that I had to remember, as I struggled through, the words I heard the Lord say to me: *"Wendy, there will be days when you will wonder if I am really here, and you will remember this and know that I AM."*

I later ran into my pastor and his wife at a local shopping center. After speaking for a few minutes, the pastor smiled and asked again, "So how are those sinuses doing?"

"They're still great; thanks for asking," I replied.

"Do you realize that was ten years ago?" the pastor reminded me.

"Oh my!" I exclaimed. "Has it been that long?" We both laughed in amazement as I confirmed that, indeed, I had not had a sinus infection since then.

I recorded this awesome healing and wonderful gift from the Lord in my journal, just as I had written down so many other blessings from times past. I kept a special journal just for writing down all the times I would see God show up each day. Each newly recorded log usually started with, "Dear Lord, thank you for ..." followed by words of gratitude and expressions of love to the Lord for all he had done and continues to do and be to me. I found the more I focused on his love, the more I noticed its existence.

Another example of writing in my journal that finished with a moment of awe toward my Lord, as recorded below, goes like this:

January 1, 2002

The clock would soon be striking midnight and an entire city of people from far and near were packed together in the middle of the streets ... It was difficult to move around. There were many bumping shoulders, with a number of them staggering drunk and shouting out various things. In spite of the craziness, everyone was eager to welcome in the New Year of 2002. The nation was glad to see 2001 go, leaving behind all the pain it had experienced with 9/11. The horrendous terrorist attacks that took down the Twin Towers, with our World Trade Center, and the Pentagon, all where thousands of lives had been lost.

Everyone was excited and hoping 2002 would bring better days ahead. Especially me, as 2001 was a challenging year in so many ways. I had experienced a lot of growth and healing through the lessons life had brought me in 2001, but much of it had been painfully earned and learned. And now, for the past month or so, I'd been finding myself in tears a lot. Perhaps the holidays were making things seem worse. I am not sure, but I've been feeling a bit lonely, a little lost, and wondering why I can't seem to find someone [who] wants to have a happy, healthy, and transparent loving relationship

with me. I've been without a partner for
five and a half years now. I've been afraid of
relationships up to this point, but now that my
children are older and more independent, I am
starting to long for someone in my life who I
can truly love and [who will love me back] ...
You know, the type of relationship that leads to
a healthy, happy, godly marriage ... Something
I have never had before. Funny thing is, it took
me over five years before I could start feeling
this way, and now that I do, I'm not sure how
to handle it at all.

Well, I had about ten minutes left before
midnight would strike, and there I was, stuck
in the middle of a mass of people with one of
my sisters and her husband. For the past five
years, I had hidden myself away at midnight,
bringing in each New Year with prayer and
asking the Lord for a special Scripture that
would help me through the New Year ahead ...
So I was feeling pretty stressed out once I
realized what I had gotten myself into. I had
agreed to spend this time with family, only to
find myself locked in and shoulder to shoulder
with a mob of people and no place to hide away.

The more I glanced at the crowd around
me, the more I realized just how alone I was. It
seemed everyone around me had someone to
embrace and celebrate with ... but there I stood
in the midst of them all, feeling even more
alone than ever before. Tears began streaming
down my cheeks. I was feeling sorry for myself.

I quickly wiped them away, in the hope that no one would notice.

I closed my eyes and said a quick prayer in my heart, asking God to be with me this New Year. I begged my Lord to please talk to my heart and give me words that would direct His focus for me going forward in this New Year. As I prayed, I could feel all my pain and a number of fears welling up inside as I cried out in my mind, *Help me, Lord! Where are you, Lord? You said you would never leave me or forsake me! I'm afraid and alone right now, and I really, really, need you!*

Then, as I cried out once again, "Lord, please talk to me and give me words of comfort," I also felt inclined to reach into my purse and pull out my little pocket Bible. As I randomly opened it up, I felt compelled to look for the words of Jesus that were written in red ink. It was so dark outside that I couldn't see anything at first, but then under the dimly lit streetlight, I began focusing on the first words I could see that were written in red print at the top of the page, which said, "Woman, why are you weeping? Whom are you seeking?" (John 20:15 NKJV).

There was God, amazing me once again with his love. Suddenly, it was clear to me; I had been weeping this past year because my eyes had been so frequently focused on someone or something other than Jesus. I needed to redirect my focus this New Year on the Lord. Then I remembered in the book of Matthew where it said, "But seek ye first the kingdom of God, and His righteousness; and all these things shall be added unto you" (Matthew 6:33 KJV). Wow, it's not that the Lord won't bless a relationship in my life, but he doesn't want that to be what I seek. He wants me to seek him first and foremost, both today and every day going forward; then he promises to take care of the rest.

I later found myself reflecting on the story in the New Testament, in John 20, and thinking about how Mary Magdalene went to the tomb where Jesus was laid to rest to find he was not there. Mary panicked and wept, experiencing another wave of grief over the loss of someone she loved dearly.

What Mary didn't realize at the time, but what she later discovered, was that what she was most desperately searching for was already with her. The risen Christ Jesus standing next to her in the garden. *How many times have I been just like Mary?* I thought. How many times had I chosen to spend my energy busily looking for someone or something else to meet my needs? How many times had I longed for love and approval, acceptance, and validation or just recognition from another, when all along, my Lord and Savior, who already was willing, waiting, and able, patiently waited for me to choose him first and allow him to love me, care for me, and fulfill my heart's deepest and most desperate desires—those things so deep that nobody or nothing could ever be able to reach, let alone fill.

Prior to Jesus's dying on the cross, as the events are described in John 20, Jesus was heard saying, "Martha, Martha ... you are worried and upset about many things, but few things are needed—or indeed only one. Mary has chosen what is better, and it will not be taken away from her" (Luke 10:41–42 NIV).

As I thought about the words of Jesus, I realized that up to this point, every man I had ever loved in my life had either left or been taken away from me. *I want what Mary has*, I thought. *That's what I want—something precious, something loving, and something that can never be taken away.*

Flashbacks of stepping into my walk-in closet after the arrest ran through my mind once again. I could see the light bulb in the ceiling of my closet that night when I had looked up, only to have it dawn on me that I should have been putting all my faith and trust in God instead of man.

The more time I spent seeking the Lord in quiet study, prayer, and contemplation, as well as listening to him speak to my heart on a regular basis, the more I experienced a validation of who I was to him and a purpose for my life. An inner trust grew as my relationship with my Lord and Savior continued to go deeper and deeper. And as it did, so grew my confidence and ability to trust in his promises and hand over my life.

A comfort and assurance came by knowing that in spite of all my imperfections and inadequacies, I still had a God who would tell me I was unconditionally loved, accepted, chosen, cared about, and intimately adored. And the more I chose to find my confidence in my Lord and who I am to him, the more secure I found myself developing on the inside and being readily able to handle the attitudes and variations of those around me.

As I sat in my favorite chair, seeking the Lord for direction one morning before work, I recognized my unsettledness, as overwhelming thoughts regarding the obstacles I would face that day lay heavy on my mind. Like waves coming onto shore, so my life was greeted with challenges, and today was no exception. I had employee and operational issues awaiting my arrival at the office that morning, like many other mornings. With my eyes closed in prayer, I said, "Oh Lord, I know that you love me, and you promise the comfort of your Holy Spirit to be with me through these ordeals, so why do I feel like I am trying to survive all the time?"

With my eyes still closed, a mental picture of myself anxiously wading through the middle of a minefield came to me, and I thought, *Yes, this is exactly what it feels like!* It was a never-ending field of rough and rocky clumps of dried dirt, lacking vegetation, and all I could see were the rounded tops of mines protruding from the ground in every direction. I was trying desperately to walk thought the minefield without stepping on one ... I was doing everything I could possibly do to survive.

I felt the Lord ask me, *"Wendy, do you want to do it your way or choose me and my way?"* Fear and panic struck me as I found myself having to examine my own heart. I cried out, "I know what my way is, Lord, so much so that I have gotten used to living from a place of survival. Somehow, it's become so familiar to me that it's almost comfortable. I don't know what your way is, God! I don't know if I can live up to it or do it. I don't know what your way means." Then, in the softest of voice, I heard these gentle words speak to my heart: *"All you have to do is choose me."*

I was surprised to find myself struggling for a moment. The truth was I had become accustomed to a life of survival; it was not a comfortable walk, but it was something I knew. I had to ask myself if I was actually willing to give up living in a "survival mode." My heart's deepest desire and longing was for the love of my Lord to take over and save me. And just like a child who holds his nose and jumps quickly into cold water to get past the shock, I took a leap of faith by deciding to let go and let God be the one in control. I cried out, "I choose you!"

As soon as I said, "I choose you!" the picture in my mind changed instantly, and I saw an image of myself standing in the middle of a lush and beautiful garden. It was located on a bluff overlooking the minefield down below, where I had once been standing in fear, tears, and worry. I unexpectedly felt safe, and my heart was at peace—quite the opposite of the anxiety I had felt before saying yes to the Lord.

I quickly saw that I was not just made to survive, but in Christ I was made to thrive. And just as the lush garden around me was blossoming, so was my heart overflowing with God's love and compassion for others who were trying frantically to get through their own minefields. With a mental picture of the Lord standing behind me and prompting me to reach out and help others, I saw myself extending a hand of hope down toward the minefield, eagerly helping to pull up others who were stuck in the same desperate trap of trying to survive.

This prayer time with the Lord was another pivotal turning point for me. God was teaching me that I always have a choice, at any given moment, to trust in the circumstances or to put my trust in him. He also showed me there were many others who needed hope as well, and my heart was filled with compassion for them. I quickly realized that making an instant choice of God and his will and way over my life and circumstances, my heart was in a place of peace, comfort, and rest. Trusting in the Lord over my circumstances, no matter what they might look like, became more natural as time went on, and when things seemed scary, I would ask the Lord to fulfill his promise, as it is spoken of in Romans 8:28, where he says he can work it for good.

Obeying the Lord was my deepest desire, and each time I acted on that desire, I realized it was a way of showing my love and appreciation to my Lord. It all started with trust. In time, the overall worries in my life began to seem smaller as my hope in the Lord grew bigger. Through my daily choice to ask God to take over and be the one in control of my life, I saw the effects of blessings for obedience as I put my faith and trust in God. I made sure I started each workday in prayer and continued to pray throughout the day for direction, discernment, guidance, and wisdom. I don't think there are enough words to describe how many times I felt the Lord's covering and protection, favor, and mercy, enabling me to head off a problem, come up with a solution, or find a new and improved way to work through a situation, due to answered prayer.

A couple of years after my minefield experience, I was grabbing my bags before heading off to the airport. I felt the Lord tell me, *"Wendy, put a copy of the book* You Are Special *by Max Lucado in your shoulder bag with you."* This is a children's book I had earlier felt the Lord direct me to purchase and give to particular children who were facing difficult circumstances in their lives, like those receiving care in a children's hospital or others who were suffering through the divorce of their parents. There were even a few adults suffering from self-esteem issues with whom I felt led to share it.

Over time I had learned to trust and follow not only the leading of the Holy Spirit but also to eagerly wait in awesome expectation for the Lord to prompt me to do something. On this particular day as I walked through the airport, I found myself looking at the children waiting, wondering to which one of them the Lord might want me to read or even give the book. Each time I saw a child, I would ask in my heart, *Lord, is this the one you want me to share the book with?* But each time I asked, I felt the answer was no. *Okay,* I thought, *perhaps you want me to wait, and you have something else in mind.*

As I waited to board my plane, I saw a young man in military fatigues sit down just a few seats away. I noticed how upset and troubled he seemed as he talked on his cell phone and squirmed about in his seat. As he ended the call, he smacked his face into the palms of his hands and slowly slid lower in his seat with a look of total despair.

My heart was filled with compassion, so I walked over to him and said, "Hello, soldier. I want you to know how much I appreciate you and all you do for our country. Could I buy you a sandwich or something to eat while you wait?" The young man looked up and a slight smile began to appear. He thanked me for my comment and admitted he was hungry. I was able to convince him to let me get him something to eat.

When I returned with his sandwich, I felt the Lord prompting me to sit down and begin a conversation. "What's your name, soldier?" I asked.

"Ricky," he replied.

"Well, it's nice to meet you, Ricky. Where are you headed?"

Ricky said he was flying to his in-laws to see his wife, who had just moved into her parents' home a few days earlier with their four-year-old son and newborn baby. Ricky was being deployed to Iraq for the second time and was to finish his last year of service there. I could see the agony in his face as he told me he was going to his in-laws' house to tell his family good-bye. Ricky explained how difficult it was to leave his family again, especially with a newborn baby. He was grateful his wife's family was there for them, but I could see layers of fear and sadness unravel as we spoke.

"You know," Ricky said as he grabbed his forehead once again, "every time I go home, I always bring a gift to my son. This is the first time I don't have a gift for him. I feel so terrible, like somehow I have totally let him down."

Just as I heard him say he didn't have a gift for his son, I felt the Holy Spirit speak to my heart and say, *"This is who I had you get the book for."*

"Ricky," I said with a smile as I opened my shoulder bag and pulled out the book, "I think I have a solution to your problem." I handed it to him, and he flipped through the pages.

"This is really nice. Are you sure?" he asked with a surprise on his face. I explained the earlier prompting I had felt from the Lord, and Ricky gratefully accepted the book. We wrote his son's name—Noah—on the inner cover, showing that it was a gift from his daddy.

"You know, Ricky," I said, "God knows what you are going through, and I think he also wants you to know he loves you. He cares about the details in your life."

A little smile started to show on Ricky's face when I asked him if he'd like me to pray for him. "Sure!" Ricky said. "I'll take all the help I can get." As he closed his eyes and bowed his head, I gently laid my hand on his arm. Then I began to quietly pray for him, asking God to comfort his fears and bless his family.

When we finished praying, I said, "Ricky, while I was praying for you, I kept seeing a picture in my mind of you returning home to your family after completing your tour. And I saw you in a career where you are helping many people. I truly sense God has good plans for you, and you will return home to your family, where you will make a positive difference in many lives." A peaceful rest began to settle over Ricky as the words brought consolation to his soul and gave him hope for his future. "So Ricky," I asked before heading back to my seat, "once you get to Iraq, what will you be doing there?"

Ricky slowly looked down for a moment and then lifted his eyes to respond. "I am a mine sweeper. I walk out ahead of the tanks on foot, searching for mines."

Instantaneously, flashes of the vision in my prayer time—when I'd seen myself desperately trying to survive as I walked through a minefield—flooded my thoughts. I had felt the Lord tell me all I had to do was choose him. Fear had caused me to freeze in my tracks, whereas choosing God and deciding to trust in him released a newfound freedom to move forward confidently and courageously as I put myself and my loved ones in his hands.

Ricky had just made a choice. He said yes to prayer and yes to the Lord and God's intervention, which gave hope for his life, for the family he would be leaving behind, and for his safe return after fulfilling his duties. When I first approached Ricky, he was filled with fear and anxiety that seemed to paralyze his very soul. But after prayer, a calmness, a look of peace, and a spirit of hope spread across his face. *That's exactly what choosing to trust in God over your circumstances looks like*, I thought. *No matter what you are going through, you are not alone. Our God is an awesome God, and he will work it out.*

"I am quite positive," I told Ricky with a smile, "that my running into you today was not a coincidence but most definitely a divine appointment by God. First, God prepared me with a book for you and your son, and now, here he is, sending you words of hope to hold on to." As I said good-bye, I could not help but leave one last word of encouragement, reminding him to keep choosing God and putting his faith and trust in his Lord and Savior, the one who died on a cross for him personally and who rose again to give him life. "Our

God is with you right now to help you along the way and to care for your family through the difficult days ahead, just as he has done for me so many times."

Each time I reflect on the kindness of the Lord and the intimately compassionate heart he has, I find myself overcome by the love of the Lord and how graciously he pours it down on me as well as others. While in prayer one day, I asked, "Lord God, I love you so much, please tell me: how can I love you back?" And I felt the Lord answer me with, *"Trust me, Wendy. That's how you can love me back—by choosing to trust me."*

Chapter 19

Beyond Broken

As I stood waiting outside the auditorium door, I felt fearless, yet I wondered, *How can that be?* My eyes kept glancing toward the man waiting in line right behind me—he was to speak after me, a highway patrolman from the same academy where the arrest took place eleven years earlier.

I had been invited to speak at my state's Annual Law Enforcement Volunteer and Coordinator Conference regarding communication skills I had learned and successfully used in business, as well as what I had enjoyed sharing and teaching to many others due to my passion and personal need to learn how to speak up and speak out.

It was not until after much prayer and a confirmation from the Lord that I ever agreed to speak here. I would be teaching over six hundred volunteers and coordinators the techniques on how to navigate through difficult conversations, as well as teaching listening skills that would assist them in their everyday lives.

As I waited, it dawned on me that the officer in line next to me did not know who I was or that I had walked the grounds of his place of employment many times over. *This is amazing,* I thought. *All of the past feelings I usually experience, like anxiety and pain, which flare up inside me at the sight of a law enforcement uniform or emblem, have somehow disappeared.* I realized I was standing in a calm and confident stillness. I experienced a renewed sense of empowerment and love of the Lord in place of fear and anxiety.

I remembered—and was embarrassed when I thought of it—how Emily and I would lift up our hands like cat's paws and say "R-r-r-r-r-r" at the sight of law enforcement personnel. Now, I felt more inclined to pray for the officer, which I did immediately in my heart. I asked the Lord to be with him and assist him in his presentation, praying it would go well for him and be a blessing to all who heard it.

The contrast sent goose bumps up and down my spine. I realized over the past eleven years, I had experienced major healing on the inside, but I also now desired the well-being and mercy of God to take precedence over the things that used to be a threat to me. I was totally astonished. The words "on earth peace, goodwill toward men" (Luke 2:14 NKJV) took on an even deeper meaning, and I could once again see that the gift of Christ is what changes the hearts of men—and in this particular case, mine.

After I finished speaking to the volunteers, one of them came up to me in the hallway and said, "You may have just saved my marriage."

"In what way?" I asked, a little surprised.

"Well," he answered, "I finally get it. I finally understand what my wife's been trying to tell me all these years."

I smiled and thanked the Lord for his hand over the training as I walked outside to grab some fresh air, only to find the parking lot and the streets around the community center filled with every department type and variety of law enforcement car you could imagine.

As I stared at the mass of cars, I wondered what the citizens in the community must be thinking. And then it dawned on me. This annual conference, which I had traveled hundreds of miles to attend, was held in the same little town where Lawrence was living when we first met.

In God's absolutely perfect timing and through a most compassionate and merciful gesture, the Lord showed me I had made a complete circle of healing in this area. In this perfect time and place, I experienced seeing myself as manifestly healed on the inside from this particular pain and anxiety of my past, but God also helped me realize this truth in the exact location where it had all once begun. This was yet another moment, like so many other times, where I could see God gently loving me.

By the time I left the conference and arrived home, I was in awe due to the transitions I continuously saw taking place in my life. Looking back over time, I could see how the Lord's continuous acts of kindness and unfailing love had slowly rid me of my past fears and worries, hang-ups, and pain. Each one was replaced with a courageous hope, an undeniable faith, and a relentless trust in him, all due to his merciful, loving kindness and unmerited favor.

I walked in the front door and plopped down in my favorite chair, exhausted from travel yet happily reflecting on the amazing love I had experienced from the Lord at the conference. Then the thought hit me: *But why, Lord? Why do you love me so much, and why would you want to use someone like me? Look at my past! Look at the choices I have made that caused so much pain to others. And look at how many times I still continue to make mistakes. Tell me how, Lord—how could you ever want to use someone like me? I am so far from perfect. I am still so broken.*

My eyes closed involuntarily as I spoke these words. Tears ran down my checks with each new question. I was humbled by my unworthiness yet filled with thanksgiving that my God would ever love me so much. As my eyes remained closed, I unexpectedly saw a picture of myself in my mind. I was holding a ceramic tile in my hand, and words were written on that tile: "My parents divorced, and my dad moved away when I was six years old." The tile slipped from my hands and crashed to the floor, shattering into a thousand different pieces. Suddenly, there was another tile in my hand with new words written on it: "When I was nine, a boy pulled down my skirt on the school playground in front of the other students." That tile also fell from my grip and shattered, but it was replaced with another tile. "I ran away from home at age fifteen; I wanted to end my life." I flinched in agony at the memory, and then once again, the tile slipped from my fingers and went crashing to the ground.

One by one, each unfortunate moment in my life—the mishaps, the unfaithfulness, the unkind and detrimental choices of those around me, as well as my own choices that did not turn out as I had expected—was reflected on each new tile that uncontrollably slipped from my hands and crashed to the floor. Things surfaced that had not crossed my mind in many years. Each new tile brought to memory painful moments of sorrow and regret, abandonment, abuse, disrespect, shame, and disgrace. Each new tile told a story of how I saw myself as an unwanted failure, completely soiled, and totally unworthy.

There was my life in a huge heap of broken tiles, scattered across the floor before me. "Well, there you go, Lord," I whispered through tear-drenched lips. "You just showed me all the reasons why you could never really use a person like me. I'm a conglomeration of life's shattered dreams and broken promises."

With my eyes still closed, I was surprised to see the hands of God reach down from heaven and pick up the entire pile of broken pieces. Then, with his love as the mortar, he reformed the entire mound of broken pieces into the most beautiful mosaic vessel, one more beautiful than anything I had ever seen. Even the smallest of flakes were mixed into the mortar and encased in his love.

"The Lord is close to the brokenhearted and saves those who are crushed in spirit." —*Psalm 34:18 (NIV)*

"In him [Jesus] all things hold together."
—*Colossians 1:17 (NIV)*

God was showing me in this very moment there was nothing so broken that his love could not put back together. He had taken every heartrending event and every devastating and regrettable moment of my life and transformed them into a vessel for his use and a place for his love to reside. He had taken all the wrongs and turned them for good that my pain would no longer be in vain but could be used to help others.

The painful things which had happened, the unhealthy choices that had led me down such a pitiful path, and the merciless choices of others that had thrust me to the ground, breaking and crushing my self-esteem and confidence, had been gathered into my Father's hands and made anew. The old tiles that were once flat and hopeless were reshaped into something useful and beautiful—a vessel with a new identity that came with a birthright and special adoption papers, telling me I belong to the King of Kings and emphatically confirming that I am forgiven, and I am wanted, loved, adored, and chosen. It was in this moment that I became convinced I would no longer be defined by the words or thoughts of those around me but by the very One who created me.

I was amazed as it dawned on me that I never again had a suicidal thought or desire to give up after I first experienced God's loving me. The agonizing hopelessness that once had such a tight grip on me was entirely replaced by the Lord's sustaining mercy and grace. My heart had been changed. I was a new person inside.

"I will give you a new heart and put a new spirit in you." —Ezekiel 36:26 (NIV)

The initial miracles I felt from God grabbed my attention, and the ongoing wonders kept my heart's song leaping in thankful awe. But it was the day-to-day quiet time, spent alone with my Lord, which filled my mosaic vessel the most. During these moments, whether reading his Word, praying, or just listening, I found myself repeatedly surrendering my heart to God and seeking him first. I was completely refilled with his peace and joy as I invited him to stay, to reside in each day of my life, and to oversee every action, both large and small, allowing him to be in the driver's seat of my life's journey.

The remarkable thing is that the more filled up I am with God's love, the more I see God using me as a vessel of love for him to pour out on others when I least expect it. Sometimes I am not even aware of it in the moment and discover his work through me much later. I think this is because when I am filled up with the love of my Savior, it somehow spills out through a simple smile, a word of encouragement, or a kind gesture in passing. This thought reminds me of the day I reached out to grab a paper towel in the woman's restroom, and Heidi, a friend from church, walked in.

"Oh, Wendy," she said to me, "I ended up praying for a woman you invited to the church conference last night. She had the most amazing experience of God's love as it flooded her to overflowing when she invited the Lord into her heart and into her situation."

I looked surprised as I answered, "I have to admit I don't really recall inviting anybody. Are you sure it was me?"

"Well, I thought it was you," Heidi said with a smile. "The woman said the reason she found out about the conference was because of a woman named Wendy who came climbing out of the bushes and invited her. You're the only Wendy I know, so I figured it must be you."

"Oh no, it couldn't be me!" I exclaimed. "I don't climb in bushes! It must have been another Wendy."

"Well, okay," Heidi answered, "but I could have sworn it was you, especially from the description she gave. The woman I prayed for said she and two other women were taking a walk a few days earlier when suddenly, down a steep embankment of bushes, they heard a woman screaming and warning them to look out below. She desperately tried not to slip and fall on top of them as she came flying down toward the sidewalk."

I instantly pictured the scene Heidi was describing, and it made me laugh, but then I realized I was laughing at the actual memory coming back to me.

"Oh my!" I said. "You know what? I think that was me." I giggled and added, "I guess I do climb in bushes after all!" We both burst into laughter.

It had been such a beautiful day just the weekend before that I decided to take a walk to where Emily was working and surprise her on her lunch break. For the first time ever, I cut across the townhome complex instead of using the main entrance, only to find myself staring down a thirty-foot slope with bushes all the way to the sidewalk. My shoes were slipping, so I leaned forward and ran at an angle. It was all I could do to keep upright. By the time I reached the bottom, I was smack in the middle of three women taking a walk. The almost-collision started a conversation, along with a lot of laughter and a description about the position in which I landed after skidding down the embankment.

"Do you live near here?" I asked the ladies after we all finished laughing.

"Two of us live just a mile up the road," one of the ladies answered as she pointed to an older woman, "but Jessica here"—she pointed to a young lady—"is visiting. She's staying with me while she sorts some things out."

Jessica glanced at me and then turned her face downward, as if to watch where her feet were walking as she divulged, "I am separated from my husband right now. Lynda was kind enough to take me in. I don't know what I am going to do. It all seems so hopeless right now."

"There is always hope," I exclaimed. "Do you know the Lord Jesus Christ?"

"Well, as a matter of fact," Jessica answered, "I just started going to church with Lynda."

My heart was filled with compassion as I said, "Jessica, I have been in your shoes, and if it had not been for the love of the Lord and his hearing my cry for help and rebuilding my life after all had been swept away, I would never be where I am today, nor would I have the ability to boldly stand in confident peace, knowing I have a God who loves me unconditionally and who will never leave me or forsake me."

A tear fell from Jessica's cheek as she turned to look at me. At the same time, a still small voice inside told me to invite Jessica to the "Father Loves You" conference being held at my church the following weekend. "Jessica," I said as I reached into my purse to pull out the flyer I had received earlier that day, "there will be a conference next weekend at my church. The pastor will share his personal story of how the unconditional love from his Father in heaven filled a void that only God could fill and how that experience changed his life forever. I know the message could bless you immensely, just as it did me. Here's a flyer on it, if you'd be interested." I handed her the paper.

By this time, we had arrived at the corner where I would say good-bye to the ladies. Our entire conversation took place within a block and a half, but in God's perfect timing, it was all that was needed to pour out new hope to Jessica as she addressed her challenges.

In the end, Jessica went to the conference and invited Christ to be her personal Savior. She soon found out she was no longer alone in her circumstances and that in the midst of her brokenness, she was also forgiven. Jessica's life changed that day as she experienced the unfailing love of her heavenly Father and the promises from God that he would help her through the difficulties which lay ahead by rebuilding a new path. I later heard through others that Jessica's marriage had been reconciled.

I have learned that with God, anything is possible, and if I am willing, even if that means getting out of my comfort zone, he will direct my path and use me as his vessel—like the time I felt the Lord leading me to act on something that went completely against my own better judgment and where I found out God had such a bigger plan in mind.

I was standing at the gate at the airport, waiting to fly home after a two-day women's retreat in the mountains. This particular airline did not have prior assigned seating; tickets were grouped into differing waves of boarding, based on when you first checked in or printed your ticket. Since I'd been without access to a computer, I was left to pick from the few unwanted seats remaining after everyone else boarded the plane.

As I stood there waiting, I noticed a man dressed in business attire, who stood much taller than those around him, and from the back side I thought, *What a tall, dark, and handsome man.* Then he turned his head, and I could see the look on his face—his mouth was turned down, and he looked angry as he seemed to be scoping out the conditions in the terminal. *Wow,* I thought, *he's not really very attractive after all.* I wondered how such a nice-looking man could look so "not nice." *Well, one thing is for sure,* I decided. *I don't know where I'm going to sit on this full plane, but it will not be next to that man!* After having two wonderfully relaxing days in the mountains, I didn't want to finish my trip next to a grump.

The people began to board the plane, and I saw the tall man enter with the first group. I was in the third group, and when it was finally my turn, I stood with my ticket in hand at the end of the line, I felt the Lord speak to my heart, admonishing me for my earlier thoughts about the tall man. *"Wendy, do you know this man's story or what is causing him to seem angry?"*

The question stopped me in my tracks. *Oh Lord,* I answered in my heart, *I am so sorry for being judgmental. You are right, Lord. Please forgive me. I don't know that man or what he is going through, but you do, Lord. So whatever he is facing in his life, will you please bless him and help him? Please pour your love on him, and let him know you are with him. Thank you Lord.*

I was humbled in that moment, which was followed by a sense of peace, knowing my unkind thoughts had been forgiven, and the Lord loved me enough to bring this human weakness so quickly to my attention. *Lord*, I said in my heart, *I am sorry for my earlier attitude, and I want you to know I will sit wherever you want me to sit. All you have to do is tell me what you want, and I'll do it. I love you, and I'll just put my trust in you.*

The line moved forward, and I handed my ticket to the airline employee checking us in at the gate. As she took it from me, I felt the Lord speak to my heart once again. *"Wendy, I want you to take the first empty seat that you come to when you enter the plane."*

Okay, Lord, I responded in my head. *I'll do whatever you ask. I'll take the first open seat that I come to.*

I waited patiently as the other passengers slowly moved through the Jetway until finally reaching the door of the plane. I paused for a moment to glance across the seats and find the first empty one. *Oh no, Lord, not him!* I thought as I realized the first empty seat was right next to the tall businessman with the growl. I took a deep breath. *I am going to do it because you told me to. I am willing to be uncomfortable. You must have something better in mind here. I just hope you let me know what it is really soon!*

After takeoff, the tall man turned to me and asked, "So where are you heading?"

"I am just heading home after joining my sister and her church friends at a two-day woman's retreat in the mountains," I responded.

"Oh," the man replied, "a friend of mine from work has been trying to get me and my wife to attend a marriage retreat through his church for the past six months, but it never seems to work out. And to be honest, I am not all that interested in going, but my wife keeps bugging me to go with her. Our marriage has been a little strained these days, with some problems we are having with our kids and all the traveling I do."

"I am sorry to hear that," I responded. "What line of work are you in that requires so much travel?"

He explained his position as vice president, overseeing multiple stores for a well-known national chain of steakhouse restaurants. "I have over two thousand employees to manage," he said, and then he asked, "So what do you do?"

I told him my similar title in the health care industry. "But," I said, "I don't have nearly the number of employees or the territory to cover that you do—although I have been doing more travel of late. I've flown to the state capital over a dozen times in the past year to meet with policy makers. I get what it's like to oversee business operations and the demands that can weigh you down. As a joke, I sometimes tell people I am a firefighter when they ask what I do. After they give me a look of surprise, I admit with a laugh that it's because sometimes it feels like all I do is put out fires all day."

I saw the man shift toward my direction and then lean forward in his seat, as if he just realized he was sitting next to someone who might be more understanding of his predicament than he first realized. "You know," the man said, "I feel really bad for my wife because she is left home to deal with our kids alone when I'm gone. Right now, we are having a particularly difficult time with one of my sons. We've taken him to a doctor, and my wife has both of us seeing a counselor, but I just don't get it. I don't know how to communicate with my son at all. He's easily angered and can get so defiant."

Before I knew it, we were deep in conversation, and although the plane was loaded to full capacity, I didn't seem to notice anyone else on the plane. After he shared some specific challenges he was having in attempting to communicate with his son, I shared some of the simple communication techniques I knew, even challenging him to focus on what the true needs were, rather than the emotions that were hiding them.

The gentleman expressed gratitude for the information and said, "I am going to try this when I get home tonight. So you must tell me ... how did you learn these techniques? You seem to have such an amazing passion for it."

This new question led our conversation down a path that unexpectedly ended with my sharing my story with him—of how God heard my cry for help and turned my nothing into something, my survival mode into living, my brokenness into healing, my fear into faith, and my grief into gratitude. He saw how my life was changed by the love of God, and he wanted the same thing too. He decided he would take a chance and invite God into his own heart and life and into his marriage and parenting.

Five minutes before landing, we prayed together in the middle of an airplane full of people while he chose to give his heart to Jesus.

"Dear Lord God," he repeated after me, "I have tried doing things my way, and it isn't working very well. I want to choose you and do it your way now. I believe Jesus died on the cross for me and rose from the grave that I might be forgiven and have eternal life. I am ready to receive your love and be called your very own. Jesus, please wash me clean and forgive me now. I welcome you into my heart. I want you to be my Lord and Savior for the rest of my life. Please fill me with your Holy Spirit and guide my life from this day forward. In Jesus's name, amen."

Tears ran down his checks, and he held a napkin to his face, overcome with joy to the point that he could not speak. When it was time to disembark from the plane, he leaped to his feet with joy, and I could tell he could not wait to tell his wife the good news.

As I walked behind this man through the terminal to the baggage area, he seemed to stand even taller, and the transformation was astonishing. This was most definitely not the same man I saw entering the plane over an hour ago. This was another man—a man filled with hope and who walked with a spring in his step and a smile on his face that went from one ear to the other.

As I leaned down to pick up my luggage from the conveyor belt, I thought, *Okay, Lord, I admit it. Not only were you right about where I should sit, but you also had something better in mind, so much more than the gentleman or I could ever have imagined. And you know what else, Lord? I'm thinking I may have been blessed more than the man on the plane, because knowing you would choose me to be a conduit of your love to help another has to be one of the most satisfying moments I have ever felt in my life.*

Being used by God, I found out, does not always start with a blissful or gratifying beginning, but through God's unfailing compassion and masterfully orchestrated timing, it can turn very quickly into a heartwarming ending. This thought reminds me of yet another time in when I had to hold on to the yellow raft and not let go—where standing in God's promises was imperative to get me through the storm, and where my very own difficulties became the one bridge that brought hope to another ...

As I hung up the telephone, a streak of panic ran through me. This was the third request from the breast center for more tests. This call was for the purpose of scheduling a double biopsy. "What if it's something serious?" I cried. *Who will be there for my children? I am the only one they really have. They need me here. I can't have anything wrong! How will they get along without me?* These thoughts went screaming through my mind as a wave of fear came crashing down upon me, sending yet another tile of my life hurling to the floor and crashing at my feet. Thoughts of helplessness struck, and I turned to my Lord for help.

I knew this was a time in my life when I would need the help and support of others alongside me. My eyes quickly glanced toward the clock. *Oh good,* I thought, *it's almost lunchtime, and I can head to the church for prayer.* As it turned out, this day was one of two days in the week when a group of volunteers made themselves available to pray for anyone who came into the church for prayer.

The two women who prayed for me that day also offered to drive me to my appointment at the breast center the next day, which was such a blessing—not so much for the transportation but more so for the moral and spiritual support they provided. They continued to pray for me during both procedures, which took over an hour to perform. They even took me to a coffee shop afterward and made sure I knew they were available to be with me for any other needs. It was such a gracious thing for them to do and an answer to prayer, as I felt God loving me once again through them both.

That following week was the longest of my life. From the time I was called in for the biopsy to the day I found out the results, I experienced all the steps we naturally go through when confronted with a life-threatening ordeal. I went through denial and anger and the "what-ifs," followed by sorrow and helplessness and ending with an unforeseen sense of acceptance.

When my doctor called with the results—both biopsy results came back benign—my relief was almost more than I could contain. I had to take a few deep breaths, and as I did, I closed my eyes and thanked the Lord once again for being with me through it all and for providing the multiple levels of care and compassion he'd sent to me.

I definitely walked with a lighter step, and my heart was filled with a joyful relief that followed me out the front door. I had important business letters to mail, so I left the office early in order to get to the post office before it closed. I dropped off the letters, but before heading home, my eyes spotted a health food store across the street. My mouth started watering for one of their freshly made vegetable juices from their juice bar, so I turned in the opposite direction from my home and headed over to their parking lot instead.

It was such a beautiful day. As I walked into the store, I said hello and shared a smile with everyone I met along the way. After ordering my juice, I walked up and down a few aisles while waiting for my order to be ready. As I checked out with the cashier, I thanked him and wished him well as I turned to the exit door.

"Hey, you! Angel lady!" a voice called out from behind me. As I turned around, a woman hurried through the doors in my direction, shouting, "Yes, you!"

I looked around to see if she was talking to anyone other than me, but there was nobody else in sight. I decided to wait beside my car as she approached me.

"So what's with all the angels?" the woman asked as she pointed to the brooch on my blouse and the angel that was hanging from the rearview mirror in my car.

"Well, as a matter of fact," I said, "I call this car my 'angel car.'" I smiled as I looked down at the brooch I was wearing and then at the angel hanging in my car. "Yes, I do seem to be surrounded by angels today."

"I'm sorry for yelling at you like that," the woman said, "but all I knew to do was call you the angel lady. By the way, my name is Mary." Then her face became more serious, and she lowered her voice as she said, "I noticed you in the store. Somehow, I knew I had to talk to you. Your face is beaming so brightly, and your smile is so radiant. I just needed to ask you why you are so happy."

"Well, it's probably because I had some good news today," I replied. "I just found out that my biopsy results are benign. So the joy on my face must be all the thankful relief I am experiencing right now."

"Oh," Mary replied, "I was not so lucky myself. As a matter of fact, I was diagnosed with breast cancer a couple months ago. I already had been fighting cervical cancer for over two years, and I've had a couple of different surgeries. I refuse to go through any more surgeries." She closed her eyes for a moment.

My heart sank in sorrow for her. All the emotions I had experienced over the past week came flooding back. "I don't know what you are going through, Mary, but for a moment, I experienced a taste of it. I am so sorry. Can I pray for you?"

She was quite surprised by my offer but happily accepted, and we stood in the parking lot next to my car in prayer. After praying for her, we continued to talk, and she told me all about what she was going through. My heart was filled with empathy, and a much deeper understanding consumed me than if we had talked one week earlier, before my own ordeal.

She asked how I might handle her predicament if I were in her shoes, and I felt the Lord speak to my heart, prompting me to share some of my personal testimony of how God heard my cry for help and began rebuilding my life, in spite of the many obstacles that were beyond my control. I also let her know God was only a choice away and readily able to love her, help her, and be her tower of strength in time of need.

Before parting ways, I reached into the side pocket of my car door where I always kept an extra copy of the book *Prison to Praise* by Merlin Carothers. "This book changed my outlook on life," I said as I handed it to Mary with a smile. "I think it could bless you too." I reached out and gave her a hug.

"I just can't believe what happened, Wendy," Mary told me. "My running into you, and talking to you, and your praying for me and giving me this book—maybe God heard me after all."

"Oh, Mary," I responded, "this encounter today is God loving you. And I think he wants you to know he hears you and is here with you. He knows your heart and feels your pain. You are not facing this alone."

We exchanged phone numbers before parting and gave each other one final hug. As Mary climbed into her car, I heard her say, "Wendy, you have no idea."

"What do you mean?" I asked.

Mary's eyes filled with tears as she replied, "I was going to end my life tonight, but now that has changed."

I later found Mary's phone number in the bottom of my purse, so I called her to see how she was doing.

"Wendy, you are my angel," she replied and then told me how incredible she was doing. She also said she took my advice and got involved with her local church, started reading God's

Word, and was attending a home group and had friends who were praying with her regularly.

I am convinced God lined up the exact moment in time when he would reach down and touch Mary with his love and at the moment when she would be the most ready to receive it. I happened to be the one God used as a vessel that day, and just like those who had given me a smile, a word of encouragement, or a prayer in my time of need, I felt extremely humbled and blessed to be the one God chose to use that time. The most gratifying moments in my life are when God uses me to help another, and in this case, being a mouthpiece of God's love and message of hope made all I had gone through worth it. God used my pain for gain in Mary's life and was able to pour out his love on her through my being there and available at that precise moment.

Visions of the mosaic vessel and what God had done with someone like me continued to play throughout my mind. I could see all the broken pieces and how they had so beautifully come together in God's merciful loving hands. This caused me to ponder over all the people God had placed in my direct path—those who willingly poured out hope in my own time of need. I could see they too were used as vessels of his love. And through it all, as is the case for all new people who choose to invite the Lord into their lives and make him their personal Savior, we have the chance to be made anew and seen through God's eyes as forgiven and wanted, whole and unbroken.

Now I get it, Lord,
I once was blind, but now I see.

You love me God and want me to know you are
always here, that you are always a choice.
You will never force your love, but you
will always give your love.

It is the evil in the world, which forces its will on
another, seeking to control and take away one's
freedom, but that is not your way, God.

You are love, life, breath, and every good thing.
Every motion you make is motivated by love.

"You, Lord, are forgiving and good, abounding
in love to all who call to you."
—Psalm 86:5 (NIV)

And because of this, you want me to choose
you freely, putting my trust in you with every
area of my life and in every situation.

"The Lord's unfailing love surrounds
the one who trusts in him."
—Psalm 32:10 (NIV)

You want me to ask and watch.
You want me to pray, trust, and give thanks.

"Always be joyful. Never stop praying. Be thankful in
all circumstances, for this is God's will for you."
—1 Thessalonians 5:16–18 (NLT)

Because you promise, that choosing you
will be the best choice I ever make.

"'For I know the plans I have for you,' declares
the Lord, 'plans to prosper you and not to harm
you, plans to give you hope and a future.'"
—Jeremiah 29:11 (NIV)

Epilogue

I have come to the conclusion that whatever rules my heart also rules my life, and each new day brings a new choice. I can either live in fear, focusing on the possibility of another broken tile, or I can choose hope by seeking the Lord and putting my eyes on Jesus, trusting in his ability to work whatever difficult circumstances I encounter for good.

I will never forget the day it dawned on me I was no longer a victim and realized I had a choice. With God, I always have a choice. I can prayerfully request God's intervention over my life, as well as another's and especially those I love. I have found trust to be an action word, which sometimes requires waiting patiently as God honors our petitions in his perfect will, way, and timing.

I have so much to be thankful for, as my children and I are now in a good place in our lives. Soon after my son's graduation, tears of joy filled my eyes as I read a note he'd written to me on a copy of his state license:

> Mom,
> We did it! I can't begin to express how grateful I am for all you have done for me and for believing in me. Things really have worked out ... Having faith and trusting in the path

laid out in front of me has made the difficult times more bearable; that's for sure. Thank you for the endless prayers, night after night, and trusting in me that I could give this my all and not only succeed but finish in the top of my class ...

When I asked my daughter what I might share with you, the reader, to let you know how we are doing, she suggested sharing this: "We have love, family, and friends, and we find ourselves closer and stronger because of the hardships we've experienced."

"Yet this I call to mind and therefore I have hope: Because of the Lord's great love we are not consumed, for his compassions never fail. They are new every morning."
                                    —Lamentations 3:21–23 (NIV)